*I'd do almost anything if I th.
was watching.*
—Stephen Elliott

Alison Tyler can bend me over anytime.
—Sommer Marsden

Alison Tyler makes me glad to be a pervert.
—Kristina Lloyd

When we're in Tyler's world, our senses go into overdrive.
—Violet Blue

I'll submit to her anytime.
—Rachel Kramer Bussel

*Alison Tyler talks about sex in such an easy, seductive way.
She's a star.*
—Saskia Walker

Infamous, intelligent, classy, and dirty as hell...
—Jane's Guide

Alison Tyler is woman—hear her purr.
—Thomas S. Roche

Also by Alison Tyler

A Is for Amour
B Is for Bondage
Best Bondage Erotica
Best Bondage Erotica, Volume 2
C Is for Coeds
Caught Looking (with Rachel Kramer Bussel)
D Is for Dress-Up
E Is for Exotic
Exposed
F Is for Fetish
Frenzy
G Is for Games
Got a Minute?
H Is for Hardcore
Hide and Seek (with Rachel Kramer Bussel)
The Happy Birthday Book of Erotica
Heat Wave
Hurts So Good
I Is for Indecent
J Is for Jealousy
K Is for Kinky
L Is for Leather
Love at First Sting
Luscious
The Merry XXXmas Book of Erotica
Naughty or Nice
Open for Business
Red Hot Erotica
Slave to Love
Three-Way

NEVER HAVE THE
SAME SEX TWICE

NEVER HAVE THE SAME SEX TWICE

A GUIDE FOR COUPLES

Alison Tyler

CLEIS
PRESS

Published in the United States by Cleis Press Inc., P.O. Box 14697, San Francisco, California 94114.

Printed in the United States.
Cover design: Scott Idleman
Cover photograph: Eryk Fitkau/Getty Images
Text design: Frank Wiedemann
Cleis Press logo art: Juana Alicia
First Edition.
10 9 8 7 6 5 4 3 2 1

"1-900-Fantasy" by Dante Davidson appeared in *Bondage on a Budget* (Pretty Things Press, 2002); "Le Petit Déjeuner" by Jeremy Edwards appeared in *A Is for Amour* (Cleis Press, 2007); "The Princess and the Penis" by Ronald Keller appeared in *Naughty Fairy Tales from A to Z* (Plume, 2004); "Death of the Marabou Slippers" by Molly Laster appeared in *D Is for Dress-Up* (Cleis Press, 2007); "Fruits of the Forest" by Kristina Lloyd appeared in *Love at First Sting* (Cleis Press, 2007); "Not Tonight" by Mathilde Madden appeared in *K Is for Kinky* (Cleis Press, 2008); "Filthy" by Sommer Marsden appeared in *Frenzy* (Cleis Press, 2008); "Coming to Conclusions" by Andrea Miller previously appeared in *Frenzy* (Cleis Press, 2008); "The Rules of the Game" by Thomas S. Roche appeared in *Hers* (Pretty Things Press, 2003); "Appetizers" by Simon Torio appeared in *Juicy Erotica* (Pretty Things Press, 2003); "Red Light, Green Light" by Alison Tyler appeared in *Sweet Life* (Cleis Press, 2001).

Library of Congress Cataloging-in-Publication Data

Tyler, Alison.
Never have the same sex twice : a guide for couples / Alison Tyler. -- 1st ed.
    p. cm.
ISBN 978-1-57344-332-6 (pbk. : alk. paper)
1. Sex instruction. 2. Sexual fantasies. 3. Sex. I. Title.

HQ31.T84 2008
306.77--dc22
                        2008036407

For SAM,
of course.

Contents

INTRODUCTION:
I DON'T MEAN
TO BRAG

don't mean to brag. (Oh, well, maybe I do.) You see, I am in the enviable position of not only living a writer's fantasy life (I get paid to do what I love), but also living out my fantasies. For nearly fifteen years, I've been one half of a monogamous relationship—a relationship filled with extreme, kinky, crazy, never-have-the-same-sex-twice sort of sex.

How is that possible?

It's thanks to a trick I learned years ago from a friend's lover. (Yes, this was *before* I was monogamous.) His goal was to always be varied, to not fall into a rut, even when engaged in a long-term relationship. His method?

"I never have the same sex twice."

At the time, I thought he was saying he never fucked the same *woman* twice, but over the years, I've come to understand he meant something else, which is this: don't settle for the fast-food concept of pleasure—the wham-bam-thank-you-ma'am style you know for a fact will get you off every time, but doesn't leave you breathless, dying to share with your closest friends exactly what sort of sweaty romp you just untangled yourself from.

Inevitably, over the years, you *do* learn things about your partner. You know all the buttons to press, or which body parts to stroke, fondle, lick and suck. Does reverse cowgirl get you off every time? I'm not saying to forgo that position in favor of doggy-style, or telling you to never ride your man backward again. When she drops to her knees to blow you, is that the best thing you can possibly imagine? Don't stop on my account. I'm simply advising you to stretch your possibilities. To see exactly how enjoyable sex can be when you push your boundaries within a monogamous relationship.

Some readers are bound to ask: "What's wrong with never fucking the same *partner* twice?" Well, of course, *nothing's* wrong with that, and there are many fine books on how to proceed with polyamorous relationships (for instance, *Opening Up* by Tristan Taormino). But that's not what I am in or what I want. I crave the security of being with one partner—the assuredness that he will always be there for me. And yet I'm an adventurous lover. I want to test the bindings, pull on the handcuffs, and rattle the headboard in the sexual side of our relationship. I always want to look at him afterward, and think, *Oh, my fucking god that was good.*

That neatly sums up the goal I set for myself when I decided to write this guide. I wanted to share my tips for how to get that *Oh, my fucking god* feeling. But I didn't want to write a dry guide. I wanted to write a *wet* guide. Or a hard guide. A rock-hard, throbbing, can't wait to slip it in you, excuse me while I take a deep breath guide. I wanted to write a guide that would turn people on while they were reading the pages. So I've illustrated my concepts with excerpts from my all-time favorite erotic stories. And I've got favorites. Since I was twenty-three, I've been making my living by editing anthologies. Forty-five books later, I've read thousands of erotic short stories. Snippets from nearly one hundred of the hottest ones ever have made it into this book, along with seventeen full-length stories.

So how can you never have the same sex twice?

All you need is a willing, creative mind.

Here, let me show you...and get ready to *always* say *never*.

Never have the same sex twice, that is.

XXX,
Alison

1 | READY, SET, GO

Fuel Your Fantasies

*The gift of fantasy has meant more to me than
my talent for absorbing positive knowledge.*
—**Albert Einstein**

see sex everywhere I go. But really I'd see sex even if I didn't go anywhere. If you put me in a white-walled room with no doors or windows, locked me in a puppy cage, or blindfolded me with your favorite paisley silk tie, I would still see sex. How? Through my filthy imagination. I cannot gaze at a stranger without imagining what he or she might be like in the throes of passion, can't watch a TV show without envisioning the main characters fucking each other, or fantasizing about them fucking me. I can't eavesdrop in the elevator without mentally undressing the people all around me.

Wherever I am, strangers are having sex.

At least, they are in the theater of my brain.

This is why fantasies are so important. You don't need to buy a single sexy item in order to expand your erotic repertoire. All you need is a starting point, a place from which you can dive into your own sea of sensuality. Need a springboard? Here are some of my favorites:

PHOTOGRAPHER AND NAUGHTY MODEL (from my story "Flash")
I could feel her next to me. Could feel the third eye of the camera focused on me. When she bent to inspect my body, her long hair tickled the head of my shaft. Her breath made me shiver, the heat of it and the fact that her mouth was so damn close to my cock. The flash of the camera sent a shudder I could feel in the base of my spine.

Each time she took a picture, she rewarded me with a different sensation. FLASH: her mouth on my balls, cupping them both. FLASH: her tongue tracing the crack of my ass. FLASH: her insistent fingers probing me.

We went through a whole roll of film this way, with me turning, unable to touch her, bound and blindfolded. Each time the flash of the camera broke through my darkness, I grew closer to orgasm. Each time she took a step away from me, I felt myself want to reach for her, to grab her.

PRINCIPAL AND NAUGHTY SCHOOLGIRL (from "Hands On" by Ariel Graham)
"I'm going to spank you," he says." I believe in hands-on punishment."

She backs one step away from him and he catches her by the wrist, back to her side of his desk. Her mouth under his is hot. Her tongue sneaks into his mouth. Without warning he pulls away, spins her back to face his desk, and pulls her skirt up to her waist. She's wearing a lacy thong, thigh-high stockings. He strokes one hand between her legs and her skin is hot, nearly burning. The lace is wet with her desire, her inner thighs dewy. He tears the fabric moving it away and slides two fingers along her slit, feeling the wetness, the slippery want, and then he yanks her skirt all the way up, tucks it in the waistband out of his way and topples her over his desk.

"Spread your legs," he whispers in her ear and she strains, muscles cording, hands holding the far side of his desk.

The wooden ruler is lying on the blotter. He takes it up and steps back, one hand on the flat of her back. "Count," he says, and brings the ruler down, a flat, satisfying thwack against her cheeks.

DOCTOR AND NAUGHTY NURSE (from "After Hours" by Dante Davidson)

The crisp white nurse's skirt fell to the floor with a tiny whisper, followed by a slightly louder murmur from the nurse herself. I couldn't wait to finger her pussy, to see just how ready she was for me, but that wasn't part of the plan. Not yet. This scenario had to follow a strict schedule, and I would ruin everything by rushing. I watched as she let her white blouse follow her skirt, and then I stared, fascinated, as she picked up both parts of the uniform, folded them neatly, and set them on the blue plastic chair.

She didn't know that I was watching her, which made the voyeuristic experience all the more powerful. She thought that I was waiting appropriately outside in the hall for her to prepare herself. But with the door cracked slightly, I had the perfect view as she took off her bra and placed the underwire contraption with the rest of her clothes. With a gentle motion, she removed her panty hose, then slid her silky white panties down her lean thighs and dropped both of these items on top of the skirt and blouse. She stared at the pile of clothing for a moment, then rearranged the stack by tucking the panties and bra between the skirt and blouse.

How quaint, *I thought to myself.* She doesn't want me to see her panties.

All right, you've probably latched on to my secret. I like naughty. Naughty almost *anything* works for me. Stick the word *naughty* in a scene, and I am yours. But the best part about role-playing your fantasies is that you don't have to be typecast. You can easily be Dom one night, sub the next; female one night, and boy (or boi) the next. If you need more inspiration, flip through your local *Yellow Pages.* How many occupations are listed? *That's* how many possible people you can be. Or peruse the kinky *Wild Side*–type ads that appear in most local weekly papers, like the ones in my story "A Walk on the Wild Side":

I got my torrid paper out of the car and lounged on our sofa to page through it. Most of the paper consisted of ads: 900-numbers, strip joints, or personal escort services. At the end, there were four pages of personals. These intrigued me. Whole sections were devoted to different kinky lifestyles.

If you're into spanking, call Carla....

Come visit Mommy Jane's playpen....

Naomi, and her lovely, size-nine feet are back from London....

Naughty coed needs discipline....

I felt myself growing wetter as I read each mini-description.

What's better than simply *having* a fantasy? *Sharing* a fantasy. In my story "A Lesson in Seduction," the turn-on for the girl is confessing her fantasy over dinner at the crowded Rainbow restaurant in Hollywood:

"I want you to bend me over, and fuck me."

"Here?" He seemed to find the idea charming.

"Here," I repeated, and the dark-haired rocker grinned at me, and would not look away. If I was going to get fucked on this table, then he was going to have a front-row seat. He'd call out encouraging comments. Or maybe he'd get involved, his fingers reaching out to stroke my hair out of my eyes or pinch my nipples, or lean in to graze my ass. He might bite my bottom lip hard, or he might throw money on the table, as if we were putting on a show for his pleasure.

"On this table?"

"Yeah," I said, firmly. "On this table."

Nick chuckled, and I'm sure he saw the vision in his mind. I wanted him to. I wanted him to see me, stripped down and bent over, while he plunged into me from behind.

"Look, I know it won't happen at the Rainbow," I said softly. "But that's what I fantasize about."

"So tell me."

"So I am," I laughed.

Of course, everyone has his *own* fantasies. When I asked readers of my blog to share theirs in honor of International Masturbation Month (which is May, in case you want to join in), I was impressed with the variety of turn-ons shared, from stockings to piercings, from biting to playing in public. (Of course, one of my own personal fetishes is reading other people's confessions. So this was a double bonus for me!)

Nyx wrote about being the object of her friend's voyeurism:

I regularly fantasize about one of my friends. She's not always an active participant; it may just be her telling me to do something and then watching me. It's not always a scene, it's more about the feelings evoked. I might be in a dressing room, and she's nearby and can hear everything, can see the feet under the door. My heart's racing, I can't believe this is actually happening. The store clerk with the lip rings is in front of me and I'm wondering what other tattoos and piercings he has. His hands are on my waist, and my hands are in his blue-streaked longish hair. I'm biting at his piercings, and his hands are tightening before pulling me down to my knees... I look up at him as I unbuckle his belt and smile, because I've just heard the door creak a little and I know she's stepped into the room....

Isabel Kerr confided her close-up obsession with cock:

What always gets me going is fantasizing about nuzzling cock. The thought of the feel of a silky smooth cushioned edge against my upper lip... Or, the sensation of pissing in warm water, or anything really, I am so easy. And shameless.

Angell let us in on her fantasy about an old friend and a special stage appearance:

My most frequent fantasy involves my best friend of seventeen years. In my fantasy, he comes up behind me in the middle of a stage, as I'm rehearsing a monologue. His hands massage my shoulders as his breath caresses my neck. My eyes close, and my voice breaks as he presses closer to me. His hands move around my body, slowly unbuttoning my white blouse. Beneath my kilt is nothing but a G-string and wetness. In my fantasy, I don't need to wear a bra, and his fingers pull at my nipples as he grinds his hardness against my ass. His hands grab my breasts at the same time as he bites my neck, branding me. I slowly turn around, and he takes my face between his palms and kisses me as I fumble with his belt. I release him from his pants, and he's hot and hard. He can smell my arousal, and he raises my skirt...his fingers probe me....

Katie shared her version of the popular fantasy of sex on a hotel balcony:

In my fantasies, I'm a bit freer than I am in real life. I can never bring myself to talk dirty, but in my fantasies I'm really able to let go. We're on a hotel balcony in the middle of the afternoon, on vacation. He comes up behind me, pressing his bulge against me as I moan and spread my legs. He feels how wet I am, and I gladly lick his fingers clean when he puts them near my lips. Then he pulls my skirt up to my hips and teases me with the tip of his cock as I'm pushing back against him, begging him to fuck me. I bend over the rail of the balcony a little more as he finally slides all the way into my wetness. I'm moaning so loudly that he covers my mouth with one hand while strumming my clit with the other, thrusting into me until I'm fighting back screams that threaten to alert our neighbors to our naughty activities. He tells me he wants me to scream as he moves his hand from my mouth, grips my hips and begins to pound into me harder and harder.

Dakota Rebel told us how her lover is always present in her fantasy sessions:

It's always Mr. Rebel. Always. Sometimes I can see him standing over me, sometimes I can't. It doesn't matter. It's not the sight of him that gets me revved...it's the sound. His voice, so deep and harsh. Barking whispered orders at me. Telling me how he wants me to touch myself. Calling me the most deliciously filthy names. Sometimes he is so close to me that I can feel his breath on my hand as I double click my mouse. Telling me how he feels watching me. Telling me what kind of naughty things he is going to do to me after I finish getting myself off. This particular fantasy has spawned maybe the best line I have ever written and yet have never had the opportunity to use in a story: "I want you to say things to me that you don't even mean."

You see? Different person, different fantasy. Or, really,

different day of the week, different hour of the day, different minute of the hour—different fantasy.

Take charge of your own. Write them down, read them to your partner, fall into them, let them carry you away.

EROTIC FICTION

JAMIE'S GAME

Isabel Nathe

C leo knotted and unknotted the snakelike silk belt around her wrists. The belt belonged to the sumptuous gold Oriental robe tossed casually over her shoulders. Jamie was watching television, not paying attention to Cleo at all. There was a basketball game on, featuring the Lakers, Jamie's most-beloved team. Cleo would have to wait, as usual. When sports were on, Cleo found it difficult to compete.

Sighing, she returned to their bedroom and lay down on the brocade, canopied bed. Still knotting and unknotting the belt around her wrists, she stared at the heavy material above her. This was one of her favorite positions—with Jamie or without. Taking a deep breath, she pretended that she was tied down, unable to get free. She imagined that Jamie would come into the room and take advantage of her bound form.

What would he do? What would happen?

Jamie might undress Cleo slowly, sliding her nightgown up her thighs, revealing the porcelain pale skin of her belly. Jamie might nuzzle his face between Cleo's legs, bestowing upon her that most treasured pleasure. He might even make her climax slowly, urging her sweetly forward with his tongue alone. That kind of climax made Cleo soak the sheets. When she was finished, she always felt that wetness underneath her. Then, when Jamie entered her, she was wet and open, her body receptive to Jamie's huge cock.

Cleo could hear the cheering from the other room. The Lakers had scored, but when would *she* get lucky? She tied and untied the belt around her wrists again, doing the knots a little bit tighter this time. She closed her eyes. What if Jamie caught her? What if Jamie came in and took the ends of the belt and tied them for real, rather than pretend? Cleo wouldn't be able to move her hands then. Jamie might tease her, might not give her the pleasure she longed for. Instead, Jamie might take Cleo his own way. Turning her facedown, thrusting his cock inside Cleo's pussy and forcing his way in. Jamie liked to do it doggy-style, with Cleo on her hands and knees facing away. He liked to wrap his fist in Cleo's hair and pull.

The thought made Cleo very wet. She could imagine being facedown in the pillow, not really screaming but close. She liked the thought of being taken, of being forced to comply, her wrists tied, Jamie's firm hand on the back of her head. The image made her so wet that she considered relieving the throbbing need between her legs, untying herself and rubbing her clit between her fingers until she came.

Another cheer sounded from the study, Jamie's dark, sultry voice gone suddenly deeper with excitement. Cleo untied her wrists and then brought the belt between her legs, pulling on the loose ends so that the gold coil of fabric pressed firmly against her cunt, dividing her pussy lips and digging into her clit. The sensation made her briefly feel weak, and she relaxed into the mattress, enjoying the moment. Then she pulled on the ends of the belt even harder, rocking her hips against the wedge of material, imagining a machine that might do this for her—a machine in which she was captive, bound firmly by her wrists to a wall; a machine with a snakelike attachment that went between her legs, a coil of thick, soft fabric that was pulled in the same manner that she was pulling on the belt now. She would beg for mercy. She would plead. But the nasty thing would keep rubbing until the pressure of it made her come.

Jamie would be in charge of the machine, wouldn't he? Jamie would have his hand on the controls, making the fabric work faster and harder against Cleo's pussy. He would know from experience exactly what it took to get Cleo off. He'd use his own expert timing to bring Cleo the orgasm she craved.

Liking that thought, she removed the belt and brought it to her lips, tasting her own juices that had soaked through the gold fabric. She inhaled deeply to smell her rich fragrance. Cleo wondered how Jamie would act if she confessed her fantasies, her desire to be bound and used, pampered and abused.

She tied the belt around her wrists and untied it. In the other room, she heard the click as the television shut off. Then Jamie's voice called out, "Cleo? You still awake, baby? You ready?" And then his heavy footsteps sounded down the hall. Cleo didn't answer his greeting. With her eyes closed, she listened as the bedroom door slowly opened.

Cleo lay with the belt between her lips—it was a gag, placed there by her master, and she must not undo it. In Cleo's fantasy, her master was now servicing Cleo himself. But Jamie couldn't see any of this. He couldn't see Cleo's master or the machine with its many torturous devices, or the shackles to hold Cleo firmly, or the instruments with which to punish her.

Cleo opened her eyes and removed the belt from her mouth.

Slowly, she tied it and untied it around her wrists. Her eyes locked on Jamie's, as she wondered, wondered...

What would Jamie do?

2 | LUST, CANDLES, AMOUR

Set the Stage

Ambiance is the unstudied grace—the grace of human dignity.

—William Pahlmann

Adding a splash of Chambord can turn a glass of champagne into a raspberry champagne cocktail. That's the way to think when looking to beautify your boudoir. Sometimes, the tiniest little additions can make a startling difference.

Years ago, a friend of mine was about to reunite with a long-distance beau. He'd been away for six months, and she was excited. I was, too—for her—and suggested we set up a sexy scenario for the big homecoming. I thought we might go out together and buy lingerie, some candles, flowers—the works. She scoffed, "We don't need extras to decorate our love." Seriously. Those were her exact words.

But she is a good friend, the type to admit when she's wrong, and a week later, she took me out for coffee. "He brought me lingerie," she blushed, "and he lit candles. And there were flowers, and champagne. It was beyond sweet. The sex was..." Her blush deepened. "Unreal."

Don't be afraid to pay a little extra attention; to add a bit of ambiance to your boudoir. Anyone who's worked in theater knows that it doesn't take much to set a stage. Low-budget is the name of the game in most regional theaters, and low-budget is what we're after here.

LIGHTS

Looking for a simple way to transform your sex life? Change the lighting. If you usually make love in the dark, turn on the overhead. If it's always nighttime when you get it on, try doing it in the daylight. If you've never thought to turn out the bedside lamp, try making love in pitch blackness. Subtle changes in lighting can work magic.

Swap a red bulb for your standard sixty-watt to throw yourself into Amsterdam's Red Light District. A bare bulb can make a room (and you) seem surprisingly naked.

One of my favorite songs is "Flashlight" by Parliament. The chorus mentions a slew of different lights, and I'm fairly sure the songwriter wasn't thinking sexual ambiance when writing the words (flashlight, spotlight, neon light, stoplight, daylight, red light, et cetera), but anyone who's seen my book titles knows that I've always been a fan of twisting lyrics.

Strobe Light

What starts off as a joke in Sommer Marsden's "Disco Queen" takes on a throbbing sexual overtone:

When she opened the basement door, the music seemed to

double in volume and bright flashes of light lit the stairwell in a crazy dance of light and dark.

"Dan?" she called when she was halfway down.

The basement-turned-club was empty at first glance. The hard tile floor they loathed so much had been cleared and mopped. A spangled dangling disco ball had been suspended from the drop ceiling. And the strobe light Dan had pilfered from her parents' garage was throwing flashes of hot white light around willy-nilly. Then a man unfolded from behind the built-in bar (that they totally intended to tear down) and she snickered before she could catch herself. White suit, black open-throated top, hair slicked back. "May I have this dance, foxy lady?" Dan asked and Keely laughed at him but her cunt went soft and warm and totally ready for him at that instant.

Flashlight

A flashlight can be more than emergency lighting. It can be a tool, a toy, a brand-new way to play, as the heroine discovers in my story "Pervert":

He likes to look inside me. He likes to turn off the lights in the bedroom, get in between my legs, and shine a flashlight directly on my privates. He says he's observing the intricacies of my cunt, the gradations of color, the soft and subtle folds of skin. He watches and plays and remarks on the precise moment when I start to get dewy wet, when my hips begin to lift off the sheet and beg him, silently, wordlessly, to drop the flashlight and give me what I need.

Black Light

I missed the black-light craze of the '70s. But I can understand the appeal, as can the characters in "Fire Woman" by Sommer Marsden:

The black light springs to life and the inside of the car is now a nightclub. I can only assume this is on loan from the infamous Mac. She turns and smiles, her white teeth glowing like the Cheshire cat in Alice in Wonderland. I do feel like I've fallen down the rabbit hole, but I like it very much. Along her cleavage she has written, Unzip your pants. Show me your cock...

"Well," she says. "What are you waiting for?"

Candlelight

Burning a few candles and adding some bubbles can change a bath from something rudimentary to something transcendent, like the way the narrator in "Damask Roses" by Angelica Dillon sets the scene for her lover:

I run her a bath, next. I light candles on the ledge of the window and on the counter. When I have money, I will pour bottles of champagne to fill her tub. The bubbles will refresh her and they will make the secret, special place between her legs tingle and tickle. She'll squirm as the bubbles find their way inside her, and she'll laugh at me and touch my lips with her fingers.

When I dry her off, I will lick the champagne from the nape of her neck. I will lay her down on a snow-white bath towel and I will lap every drop of champagne from the valley of her stomach, until I am tonguing in between her lips to taste her own liquid.

She says she's fine with the cheap wine I can afford. She smiles at me when she sees the candles all around the tub, the candlelight hiding the crack in our mirror and the places in the wall where the tiles have fallen.

Or the room in Shanna Germain's "And Serpent Became Rod":

I pushed the door open. Candlelight flickered in every corner.

The room was larger than I thought. And then I realized, no, it was mirrors. Everywhere. Making a million candles, a million rooms.

Neon Light

A neon sign changes everything, as evidenced in my story "Andrew and the Blade":

We fucked in his water bed, a first for me. There was a neon OPEN *sign above his bed, and the light gilded our skin in a pale blue, reminding me of the light in some after-hours clubs, an unearthly glow.*

For a bonus round, leave the bedroom to see how sexy it can be to fuck under streetlight, as the characters do in Sommer Marsden's "Risk":

"Get in," he growled into my mouth, his lips still attacking mine.

I found the handle and pulled to release it. The inside of the car was dark. Warmer than the cool fall night air. I slid across the seat, my jeans making a slick sound as I moved. Just the faintest hint of streetlights. The interior of the car lit blue and surreal. The kind of lighting that would allow me to tell myself that I hadn't done what I was about to do. That it was all a dream.

Or to a klieg light, like in "The Big Touchdown" by Erica Dumas:

The only lights are angled shafts from one faraway klieg light. We get into the backseat and start to make out. From the second our lips touch I can feel your cock growing in your blue jeans. Our tongues intertwine as I slip my hand under your football jersey and stroke your muscled chest.

"Omigod," I say enthusiastically, "I couldn't believe it! That was so great when you caught the pass and ran fifty yards for the big touchdown!"

"Yeah?" you say, smiling, all arrogant and pleased with yourself.

I giggle. "Yeah! I was sooooo proud of you!"

You kiss me, hard, your tongue deep in my mouth as your hand touches the swell of my breast under the tight poly-cotton cheerleader uniform. Your palm gently presses my nipple as it stretches the fabric.

Once you've got all of your spotlights focused, move on to the mattress.

Bedding

Have years passed since you last tricked out your bed? Are the sheets worn thin, the pillows flatter than a failed soufflé? Perhaps it's time to scour the next white sale. Because sheets can transform a bed the way a new haircut transforms a person.

Satin sheets make an appearance in my story "Naked Is As Naked Does":

"God, you're sexy," Wes said. Once again, I'd tried to make the bed while naked. And once again, Wes had found it far more interesting to muss things up.

"I'm almost finished," I told him, leaning across the mattress to stretch the corners of the scarlet satin sheets as flat as I could get them. I knew this position made my ass look amazing, and I added an extra little wiggle to my hips as I focused on tucking in the far corner of the sheet. "Just let me—"

"Sure, I'll let you," he laughed, pushing me forward, so that I was spread out facedown on the still-rumpled ruby red comforter, and then pressing against me from behind. "I love when you do the chores naked," he continued in a soft, sexy growl.

Sommer Marsden describes the perfect sheets in "How He Likes Me":

Lately, this is how he likes me. Spread out, facedown on white linen sheets. They must be white. No other color is acceptable. A pillow must be below my hip bones, so my ass is positioned high.

He says the white shows off the black more.

"Simplicity is the key," he tells me.

White sheets. Black leather gloves. Ass high. My black hair fanned out and artfully arranged to hide half of my face. It must all be perfect before anything happens.

"You look like a painting," he says.

The scene wouldn't be the same with plaid sheets. Or flannel ones. Or ratty old leftovers from your college days. This story calls for white linens. Why not try some yourself?

In "Daddy's Pillow" by Rita Winchester, it's the pillow, not the sheets, that is key:

I hate when Christian travels. I hate the big empty spot in my bed. I hate how I don't have to wrestle him for sheets and covers. I hate how cold I get without his warm body next to me. His pillow gives me comfort. I snuggle it close and inhale deeply. The smell of his skin and his aftershave are a ghostly presence, no matter how fresh the linens.

Unable to sleep, I roll over and stare at the place where he should be. Feel that clench in my belly. That loneliness that nibbles at my insides. I pull the pillow close, hold in, smell him. The phone rings.

Music

My best, weirdest, wickedest sexual encounter occurred to the tune of "Ode to Billy Joe." There, I've said it. I've laid my soul bare. Sweet little Bobbie Gentry crooned about that dusty, Delta day, while I was bent over, getting reamed from behind. Billy Joe jumped off the Tallahatchie Bridge, while my man was thrashing me good with the worn leather of his old black belt. I don't know how it happened. I don't know why. Shouldn't we have been listening to NIN or Nirvana? The Cure or the Cult?

No, it was Bobbie Gentry.

And I'll never forget it.

So now's the time for you to peruse your vinyl, or rub the ball of your thumb over your iPod shuffle, and choose the tunes to set your mood. The scintillating thing about setting a soundtrack to fuck to is that the beat can change the encounter. You might want Marvin Gaye one day and Maroon 5 the next.

But you don't even have to know the song to have music be a turn-on, as shown in "A Girl, Two Guys, and a Sex Toy" by Kristina Wright:

I was so wet and hot, I could barely stand it. My body was throbbing in time to the base of the stereo. I couldn't make out the song, but the thump-thump-thump of the base vibrated the walls—and my skin. My clit quivered to be touched and stroked in time to that thumping base and, looking from Michael to Kevin, I decided I didn't want them to do it. I wanted to do it while they watched.

When I posted an article about sexual soundtracks on my blog, the range of favorite sexy songs that fellow erotic writers mentioned could have filled a jukebox.

"Sex-O-Matic Venus Freak" by Macy Gray, and Serge Gainsbourg. "French Kiss" by Lil' Louis. Anything with the sound of a woman moaning and a slick beat behind it. Filthy electronica for a certain louche, decadent thrill.—Nikki Magennis

I'd probably go for Ella Fitzgerald (especially a live version I have of her doing "Mack the Knife"). Tom Waits. I could listen

to Tom Waits reading a Chinese takeaway menu, and still get off on him. His voice is soaked in whisky and sleaze. He makes me want to elope with someone not to be trusted or go prowling down a neon-lit back street. "Wrong Side of the Road." Or maybe "Sweet Little Bullet." Or "9th and Hennepin." Or maybe I need to play all my Tom Waits albums before I can decide. Patti Smith, especially Horses. *PJ Harvey,* "Dress." *So whorish.*—Kristina Lloyd

Yes to Kate Bush! "Feel It," Sensual World. *And "Kashmir" and other Zeppelin. And Def Leppard. Wouldn't the world be a sadder place if we didn't have "Pour Some Sugar on Me"? Then again, I* am *stuck in the '80s: pop, rock, hair, metal, yum.*— Dayle A. Dermatis

INXS. The old stuff, of course…the way he [Michael Hutchence] would breathe at the end of a lyric, like he was all hot and bothered himself…—Gwen Masters

I also love Fiona Apple's "Criminal," and at the risk of being tremendously made fun of, there's a country song by Chris LeDoux that I think is so sexy called "That's What Loving You Means to Me." Lyrics, music, his voice—it just all comes together to really do it for me.—Emerald

It's Mozart that makes me feel the most wildly, sexually alive. Never more so than in the manic violins in his Symphony no. 25. Perhaps it's because I can't separate the music from the man and there's just something about mad genius. Chaos. Unpredictability. Insufferable arrogance that's completely justified.—Fiona Locke

From Def Leppard to Mozart, music can change a scene entirely. You might even want to fuck to opera, or *at* an opera, which is what happens in Erica DeQuaya's "Operatic Ecstasy":

Her attention still apparently on the opera, Genera slowly moved his hand from her lips and slid it provocatively over her body, over the exposed flesh of her chest and upper breasts, across the soft black velvet, then under the hem of her dress. Edward sat still, gritting his teeth, feeling hot lust pound through his veins as she urged him gently up her thigh. She wore stockings and a garter belt, rather than typical panty hose, and he didn't resist as she pushed his hand past the silken hose, to the bare, warm flesh of her upper thigh and beyond. He stopped suddenly and swallowed in disbelief.

Genera wasn't wearing any underwear.

She turned to him, a slight smile touching her lips. She moved her mouth and he saw the words forming in the dim light.

Do me. Now.

She spread her legs slightly and leaned back, closing her eyes. Edward sat for a long moment, stunned, only dimly aware of the operatic gymnastics continuing onstage. He looked at Genera, her sexy dress rucked high on her thighs, legs spread in a wanton offering, her body screaming its invitation for his touch. He wondered where all of this was coming from. Not that he was complaining. But this wasn't like her. Genera wasn't into public displays of affection; she hated even holding hands in public. Just the other day, he'd teased Genera about her reluctance to kiss or touch him in public. As a joke, he'd dared her to try to seduce him in public.

She was now apparently taking him up on that dare. He realized, suddenly, what this evening was all about and despite his sexual excitement, had to restrain a laugh.

Be careful what you wish for.

To show how completely different a beat can make a scene, there's Jolene Hui's "The Salsa Bar":

The Salsa bar was loud, and the music rang in my ears. Bright lights decorated the entire bar area and the band was dressed in zesty oranges, reds, and blues. There was an actual disco ball above the dance floor.

Olivier led me to the dance floor and pressed his body to mine. In my liquor haze I pressed my lips to his. I had no idea how to salsa but our bodies seemed to move together seamlessly. His hands went to my waist and his hips swirled. I broke eye contact to see an older woman in spandex next to the stage moving to the music. She was precise in her movements and extremely sexual. It was like a dream: the music, the lights, the woman and her fuchsia lipstick, her short gray hair slicked back against her head. Olivier pulled me out the back door where we ended up on the rocky beach. He pulled me close like we had been inside. The music echoed outside and the soft tide mingled in to create a perfect soundtrack.

However you decide to dress up your bedroom, with lights, sound, and new décor, the lust will surely follow.

BLACK LIGHT

N. T. Morley

Seeking refuge from the party, Jana had planted herself on the red velvet couch with a beer and was watching an abstract dance of glowing neon shapes on the forty-two-inch plasma with the White Stripes blaring on the stereo. Miles came up behind her.

He leaned over the back of the couch, bent down and let his arms curve over her shoulders, hands resting on her breasts. He kissed her and she arched her back, then said, "Hey!" when he began to gently finger her nipples.

"Everyone else is getting comfortable."

"Yeah, I know," she said, relaxing into the couch and letting him kiss her again. His fingertips caressed her some more and she started to wish she'd worn a bra—kind of. Her nipples hardened at his touch and she sort of wanted more; glancing around, she saw people sprawled around making out, one chick with two guys, even. Terry and Tina's parties were always like this, and it never felt sleazy. She relaxed into it and as he kissed her she even let him slide his hands down her shirt. If he hadn't noticed before that she wasn't wearing a bra, he realized it now, and seemed to approve.

She drew the line when he slid his hand down to her thigh and started moving it up, though. She was not wearing anything down there, either, and in her current mood, she'd definitely end up begging Miles to fuck her from behind on the couch, in front of everyone. Jana gently closed her thighs, kissed Miles on the lips and said softly, "Wouldn't you rather go somewhere more private?"

He disengaged from her, came around to the front of the couch, and eased himself down next to Jana, taking her in his arms.

"Yes, I think so," he said. "How about here?"

His lips on hers were just the right amount of firm and his tongue was just the right amount of soft; so right, in fact, that when his hand went up her skirt she spread her legs a little, and when he lifted her shirt to expose her teacup breasts, she let him. He bent low and began to suckle her hardening nipples; she felt a thrill as she wondered if he was going to go down on her right here, with everyone watching. She decided she was going to let him; in fact, if he wanted to fuck her, here, everyone would get to see it. They were definitely collecting some spectators, and some make-out sessions had stopped or slowed down to allow the participants to watch them. Jana felt scared but turned on; fuck it, she was going to beg him for it.

This time when he moved his hand under her short skirt she not only let him but whimpered a little, nipping at his tongue as he discovered that a bra wasn't the only thing she'd gone without.

"You little devil," he whispered as he caressed her smooth, bare pussy. He slid two fingers into her and discovered she was not only bare and shaved, but wet.

She let out a vixenish "Ah!" and snuggled her body more tightly against him, adjusting her hips to push herself onto his fingers. He thumbed her clit and she arched her back, whimpering; he pressed deeper into her and she looked up at him hungrily.

"I found a place," he said. "I think you'll like it."

"What's wrong with right here?"

"Too many spectators," he said; though plenty of people were sprawled around making out, several were eyeballing them with a mix of eagerness and distaste. "This one's more private."

He pushed his fingers more fully into her, and she gasped, whimpered, moaned softly, and said, "I'm game."

He slid his fingers out of her and brought them to her lips; she obediently licked them clean. She could never say no to Miles. He took her hand, guided her to her feet, and began to lead her out of the living room into a hallway. She was already in the hall when she realized her top was still pulled up; when she went to pull it down he put his big arm around her from behind and held it up, showing her off to everyone she passed. People paused while making out to look appreciatively at her breasts, especially as Miles fingered her hard nipples. She breathed harder with every step.

"It's official," she said. "You've made me the biggest slut at a Terry and Tina party."

He chuckled, his breath warm in her ear. "Not yet I haven't," he said, his voice like melted chocolate. "But I'm about to."

Miles led her into a back bedroom that looked totally dark from the hall. As he guided her into it, she saw that it wasn't totally dark; there was a faint blue-purple glow, and the walls were streaked with glowing shapes. A trio of partygoers—two girls and a guy, she thought—were parked on a big bunch of pillows, giggling and rubbing one another's bellies, arms, and legs with phosphorescent paint, their fingertips leaving streaks as they played. The pillows, too, were smeared with glowing colors.

The trio looked up as Miles and Jana entered; their eyes lazed over Jana's now faintly glowing breasts and they smiled.

"You don't mind, do you?" asked Miles.

"Nah," said one of the chicks, standing. "We were just leaving. Miles pulled Jana close and kissed her as the three filed past them with knowing glances. Miles got a hold on Jana's top and pulled it up farther; she obediently lifted her arms and let him pull it over her head. A sudden attack of shyness made her cross her arms over her breasts as Miles tried to caress them.

"What's the deal?" she giggled.

Miles smiled, kissed her, and pushed her back. She went easily down onto the big pile of pillows, laughing a little as she did. She propped herself with her arms behind her and let Miles watch her for a moment, thrilling at his appreciative look. She kicked off her shoes and gave Miles a smile. Miles turned and closed the door, locking it. He took off his own shirt, grabbed a ketchup bottle from somewhere, and joined Jana on the pillows. She gasped and descended into hysterics as he upended the ketchup bottle and squirted a thick stream of glowing yellow liquid onto her breasts; it was cold.

"Black light," he said. "And neon paint. *Edible* neon paint," he said, and leaned down to lick it off of her.

"Huh?" Jana giggled. "No way. Edible? Nothing like a little radium in your diet...." Miles's lips closed over her hard yellow nipple and she moaned as he suckled. She arched her back and reached down to slide her skirt off of her body; since she'd already kicked off her shoes, she was totally fucking stark naked, and she knew she was about to get fucked.

Hungrily, she reached out for Miles's belt buckle, but he guided her hand away and squirted more paint on her body.

The cold made her gasp; she wriggled under his stroke as Miles smeared the thick glowing yellow paint over her breasts, illuminating them. He continued down her belly, coating her in neon, and when he tugged gently on her thighs she obediently opened them, exposing her sex.

He reached out and grabbed the pink paint—same kind of ketchup bottle. He kissed her deep and squirted cold liquid on her thighs, smearing and caressing it all over her pussy.

"You're sure it's edible?"

"And sugar free," he said. "No artificial sweeteners—that's why it tastes so good." He slid his glowing fingers into her mouth. The taste was kind of chalky and a little gross, except she could still taste her pussy, which made her go all wet inside. She opened her legs farther, and he drew his fingers from her mouth, taking them to her pussy, teasing it open. She moaned as his fingers slid into her; she clutched him close and wriggled against his stroke. The soft glow suffused the room, Jana's breasts phosphorescing as they surged with each little moan and twitch of her body.

"And everyone can see," Miles said into her ear, his thumb working her clit.

It took her a moment to realize what he'd said; by then, he had slid three fingers into her, out, in again, then out; she'd already undone his belt buckle and had his cock out and was about to bend forward to take it in her mouth. She was moments from his cock and both of them smeared with paint, when it dawned on her what he'd just said.

"What?"

He looked puzzled. "Everyone can see," he said. "You were watching."

With one orange-glowing hand, he gestured over to the webcam propped on a tripod, pointing right at them.

Jana panicked and stood. "The television?" she said. "Oh, fuck, you are fucking kidding me."

Miles took her wrist and tugged her back toward the pillows. "I thought you knew," he said. Jana turned toward the camera, and looked down at her naked body, breasts smeared with glowing yellow paint, thighs and pussy smeared with pink.

"Sorry, I thought you knew," he said. "You were watching it."

"I couldn't fucking tell what it was," she said. "Or who it was."

Miles pulled her back onto him, and the fight went out of her as he said, "Neither can they."

She didn't have time to think about it—didn't *want* to think about it. She let him pull her into his lap and bend her over it, reaching down to finger her until she melted into his stroke. She lifted her ass high in the air and he teased her open and worked her clit; God, she wanted to fuck, and a few minutes ago she'd been about to give it up on the couch. He was hard against her, his cock hanging out and the tip as wet with precum as with glowing paint. "Fuck it," she said, and slid his pants off of him, leaving glowing streaks of light down his legs as she took his cock in her mouth and started sucking him.

His hands left streamers through her hair as he caressed her head gently; each time she looked up he was staring at the webcam, moaning with pleasure. That gave her a thrill, and when his breathing changed and she realized he would come if she didn't stop, she came off his cock, gasping and panting, and said, "Fuck it," again, then "Fuck me." She left a pink handprint in the center of his chest as she pushed him back onto the pillows, then turned around, climbing over him and spreading her legs very wide. She could feel his cock against her ass, and as she lifted herself slightly and guided it up against her pussy, she saw the wetness of her cunt making the paint run all over it. Soon Miles's cock was glowing, and as she teased herself open for him she got a visceral thrill wondering what the people in the living room were seeing. She stroked his cockhead against her opening and wriggled herself onto it; just like always, it made her gasp a little as it popped into her, then continued easily in as she settled down to take him all the way.

She felt the strain on her thighs as she began to fuck herself onto Miles's cock. "Fuck," she heard herself saying. "Do people really fuck in this position?" Miles was too busy moaning in pleasure to answer, but as she looked down at her own naked body, glowing breasts, thighs, and pussy illuminated with Miles's big cock going into the latter, she thought, *Yeah, they do, when they're getting off on being watched.* She couldn't come like this; the curve of Miles's cock deep inside her just didn't hit the right spots, but god how it fucking turned her on to see herself all aglow and exposed, naked as she fucked herself onto him with everyone in the living room watching. She could never come in public anyway, not when he'd fingered her at the movies or fucked her over the railing at the beach that one time, or when he'd gone down on her twice in that secluded corner in the backyard at the Terry and Tina party last month. That didn't make her like it any less; in fact, she liked it more, because the pleasure was purely exhibitionistic, and the physical part was just a fucking turn-on.

So she thought, as she fucked herself onto Miles—until she felt him lifting her off of him, turning her naked body over in his big arms, and flipping her onto her belly on the big pile of pillows. She stared into old fabric neon-streaked with a half-dozen colors as she obediently spread her legs and put her ass in the air, knowing she was about to get fucked. And with a mixture of panic and excitement, she understood that this was the position in which he always made her come.

She wasn't sure why—it was something about the angle, the way his cock went into her when she was opened wide and on her knees with her ass in the air, versus spread wide on her back, or riding him with her legs open facing in or facing out. All those felt incredible, but it was this position, fucked from behind doggy-style that always finished her off, even if she was trying to wait.

He got behind her, fitted his glowing cockhead to her pussy, and entered her with a sigh. She let out a sigh herself, taking him to the hilt, and she wriggled against him as he began to fuck her. She could feel the tension, the pressure of his cock hitting just the place it took to make her come; then he went up on one foot and tipped his body to the side, changing the angle. She puzzled over that for an instant, until she looked back and realized he was fucking her so the camera could see.

The smooth, easy pressure of cock to pussy was replaced by a shameless exhibitionistic thrill that made her understand that she was going to come anyway. Just in case, he reached down and began to stroke her clit, propelling her closer as she stared at the camera and thought of all those people watching, staring at her tits, her body, her spread thighs, her opened cunt.

That pushed her over the edge; her eyes rolled back and she came, moaning crazily, her lips forming a glowing O with the taste of the paint from his cock. She shuddered all over as he fucked her and rubbed her clit; her sex clenched tight around his cock and she sprawled helpless under him, her whole body suffused with light and pleasure.

He pulled out of her, rolled her over, and straddled her belly. She wrapped both her hands around his cock, eagerly prepared to jerk him off, but he wanted to do it, so he wrapped his hand over hers and stroked himself until with a cry of pleasure he shot warm cum all over her breasts, the spurts glowing, more faintly than the paint. She smeared it over her breasts, watching his cum mingle with pure light. Miles relaxed into the pillows next to Jana, kissing her, their naked bodies pressed together. Jana looked up and saw Miles's face, glowing with neon paint. Her own felt sticky.

She looked into the camera, picturing her own face, illuminated like Miles's—eminently recognizable, and brightly colored to boot.

So much for anonymity.

Jana kissed Miles deeply and spread her legs, sighing softly.

3 | GETTING TO KNOW YOU

Turn Yourself On

*Don't knock masturbation. It's sex with someone
I love.*

—Woody Allen

If you don't know what you like, how can you expect your partner to give you pleasure? You can't. Sprawling on a bed and expecting a bounty of bliss may sound nice, but having a solid starting point is key. So how do you find out what turns you on?

Jill off. Tickle your fancy. Oil your oyster. Whatever you want to call the action, this is the time to take business in hand. There are endless ways to describe masturbation, each one more humorous than the next: Beat off. Box the Jesuit. Choke the chicken. Cuff your governor. Diddle yourself. Gallop your antelope. Get ahold of yourself. Jack off. Jerk off. Jill off.

Manipulate your mango. Play with yourself. Pound off. Pound your pomegranate. Pull your wire. Pump your pickle. Pump your python. Snap the rubber. Snap the whip. Spank yourself. Squeeze the lemon. Stroke yourself. Take yourself in hand. Tickle your pickle. Toss off. Twang your wire. Wank off. Whack off. Whack the bishop. Whip off. Work off. Yank off. Yank your strap. Yank your yam.

Now, I don't know what knowing all these terms says about me—oh, hell. Sure I do. It says I'm very adept at plucking my own magic twanger, because I write about self-love all the time, like in my story "Three in One":

Slowly, so slowly, the cockhead teases its way in. I clench my eyes tight, and then the bulbous head is in me. I sigh with relief as the shaft slides easily forward.

Oh, yes. Oh, yes. I'm going to come again. This time with the cock in my asshole. I use my own fingers under my body to touch my clit while I'm getting a pounding in my rear hole. My fingers work faster; the cock thrusts harder, and then I'm there—at the finish, panting and sweating, and so high from the release that I let the cock slip from my mouth.

After a moment, I push the blindfold away, only to discover that I am alone in my bed. There are no strangers making love to me, only a few soiled dildos and a half-empty bottle of lube on the mattress at my side. I'm all by myself—but I grin when I think about tomorrow night.

When I just might go for three in one once again.

Brooke Stern's "Tales of a Serial Masturbator" looks at female jerking off from a male perspective:

He had read somewhere that academics masturbated more than anyone else. Maybe it was all those hours in the library, fighting off exhaustion and tedium with frequent trips to the bathroom, where people (bless them) sometimes left a library copy of Anaïs Nin erotica. It had been Gwen who'd first admitted to him that girls, too, masturbated in library bath-room stalls. Jackson would never look at a woman leaving a bathroom the same way again. Gwen masturbated a lot, even having some elaborate ways of strapping a dildo to a chair so she could ride it while she held a vibrator to her clit. They'd had a lot of sex at first. She had a great selection of sex toys and that was the first chance Jackson had had to try different arrangements of penetrations and vibrations. Gwen had been a little self-conscious and would have died if she could have seen herself with the pink, vibrating anal beads sticking out of her ass, the black dildo stretching her pussy lips, and the giant magic-wand vibrator on her clit, making her come over and over again. Fortunately, Jackson had blindfolded her, and she let herself enjoy her bliss while he held the toys in place so that her throbbing orgasms didn't push them out.

Aimee Nichols cleverly combines voyeurism, exhibitionism, and onanism in her story "The Window":

Cecilia likes to think that people can see in even though she can't see out. Cecilia likes to fantasize that someone's out there, watching her, as she pads around her bedroom getting ready for bed; while she lies on her bed reading at night, naked and care-fully arranged to give her imagined voyeur the best possible view. She's excited when she thinks that just by lying there, she might be the object of fantasy for some silent observer. She watches porn videos with the sound turned right up and the window open and imagines that the man she's invented, the man who's out there lurking in the bushes on her front lawn, is watching his own porno inside his head as he masturbates over her.

Cecilia mounts the windowsill, dangling her legs over onto the cool brick, and allows the air to caress her. She perches with the knowledge that she could be visible to anyone. Slowly, solemnly, and with great relish, she begins to touch herself.

But while Cecilia merely *imagines* she's being watched, Bonnie Davidson's character in "Show Time" knows for sure men are watching her touch herself:

I whimpered, moaned and squirmed some more and it was hardly an act. My pussy was hard and aching with need by the time my hand reached it. I traced a finger along the hot, wet seam in between the folds of my labia then drew the juices up onto my clit. I tickled it in little circles, gasping at the sensation and half-closing my eyes.

A quick glance confirmed my audience of one was still engrossed.

If touching yourself is a foreign activity, try doing it with a partner. In "The Masterpiece," which is one of my favorite stories by Dante Davidson, the narrator asks his new boyfriend to demonstrate his one-on-one style:

"You want me to jerk off?"

"Use your hand," I told him. "Use it the way you do when you're alone at home and it's been a long night and you need some release." I was talking through gritted teeth; I don't know why. The sound of my voice was unrecognizable to me, almost monotone, but I didn't care. I needed to see.

He slowly wrapped the fingers of his right hand around his throbbing cock. I took my breath in and held it while he began to stroke himself. I've never seen anything quite as beautiful as the spectacle of him standing naked and pleasing me with his own personal pleasure. Each stroke was a chord inside my head, a cymbal, an electric jolt.

He grew more comfortable with me as his audience and he closed his eyes and tightened his thigh muscles. I would have demanded he open his eyes at any other time, but if this was the way he did it at home, alone, solo, then I wouldn't fight him on it.

His strokes grew faster and rougher and I felt myself breathing hard and fast as if to match that speed. His hand became almost a blur, and the edge of his palm made a smacking sound against his skin each time he connected. It was something from an X-rated movie, something from my fantasy repertoire, something from a place older than time. He sucked in his breath between his teeth right before he erupted. His head went back and I wanted to go to him and hold him but I was frozen where I stood, watching.

Even if you *are* well-practiced at the art of self-love, try doing it with a partner! Nothing is quite as sexy as watching someone who is watching you back—says the girl who loves to both watch and be watched.

EROTIC FICTION

COMING TO CONCLUSIONS

Andrea Miller

t's nothing personal," I said, slipping my hand into the fork of
Nick's crotch. "Rory turns everyone down."

I unzipped his pants and his cock—short and thick with a
bulbous head—sprang out. Yes, I thought, pumping it softly, the
person who'd come up with the term *tool* must have had a cock
like this one in mind. A drop of precome gathered at the tip and
I licked it off.

"Rory's an ice queen," I continued—not quite calling her a
"frigid bitch," but leaving enough pause between strokes for
him to say it himself, with his fists clenched and his dick rock
hard.

"Every month she comes to your parties, but she never fucks
anyone. She never blows anyone or eats anyone out. She never
even lets anyone see her cunt." I was stirring up shit by saying
all this, yet that's exactly what I wanted. I wanted Nick to feel
as frustrated as I did. Yes, it was his house and so I thought he
was in the best position to do something. Something hot and

nasty that would get back at Rory for always breezing past me, turning me down. Something that would give me, even vicariously, a taste of her snatch.

Nick's cock strained up and into my mouth, his butt lifting inches off the armchair. *If I don't stop,* I thought, *he's going to shoot down my throat.*

To keep him steady, I gripped the base of his tool and then I slid my lips off of it. I had a point to make and, for it to be effective, I had to leave him dangling.

"Don't you think it's strange," I asked, just as his eyes shot open, wondering why I'd stopped, "that at every party Rory locks herself in the bathroom?" I slipped my fingers down between his legs. "Don't you wonder, Nick, what she does in there all that time?" He tilted his head and finally—finally he smiled, coming to the same conclusion I'd come to.

"Some friends have just arrived," I said, getting up off my knees. "Perhaps we'll continue this later." *Like never,* I added mentally. Nick wasn't my type; he had boring mousy hair and even in black leather he smelled of the suburbs. I turned on my heels and walked to the front room where I could hear the newcomers flirting.

I gave them both a hug and let them feel me up, but I didn't get very involved. I was too busy watching Nick and Rory. And Rory, she was doing some watching of her own. As usual, she was sitting on the sofa checking out everything that was going on in the room.

First, Rory watched a blonde and a brunette on the opposite sofa. The blonde, in white panties, was simultaneously wriggling against her own finger and eating out the brunette. The brunette had her thighs spread open, her mouth parted, her fingers knotted in the blonde's hair. She bucked her hips like she loved being seen, moaned like she loved being heard. I imagined

I was the blonde and Rory was the brunette and the fantasy was so palpable I could almost taste her slit—strong with salt and musk. Then I imagined Rory was the blonde and I was the brunette and I was filling her whole mouth with my cream.

Rory crossed and recrossed her legs and then her attention drifted to the corner where a man was greasing another's crack, slipping in first one finger, then two, three...and while his hole was being stretched ever wider, the man getting fucked stifled his moans by jamming a third man's cock in his mouth. I wondered if the threesome was making Rory as wet as it was making me, but I couldn't tell—her face was a perfectly composed blank. Her scarlet lipstick, unlike mine, was still smooth and glossy.

Nick walked by and headed down the hall to the bathroom. Was he going to hide in there and try to catch Rory in the act? Hoping so, I squirmed in my seat. Rory ignored him as he passed and her gaze, with mine in hot pursuit, flicked to the TV. It had a massive screen that dominated most of one wall, and it was playing one of Nick's porn movies. I wasn't sure if I'd seen this one at a previous party or not, as all his movies had a similar look and theme. He liked to see women with fake titties and bleached hair and he liked to see them beg for the dubious privilege of blowing some jackass.

"Please," the porn bitch pleaded. "I'll do anything if you let me suck you."

After about twenty minutes, Nick came back from down the hall. Maybe he'd given up waiting for Rory, I thought. She was still sitting on the sofa, untouchable in a full-body catsuit zipped up to her collarbone. And yes, she was still watching everyone else fuck. Now her attention was directed to a straight couple on the rug—to the woman straddled over the man's face, her mouth stuffed with his cock. His fingers were jamming into her hole each time he flicked his tongue across her clit. For a split second

Rory's lips parted. Then she pursed them hard and stood up. My stomach flipped, hoping she'd swing her gorgeous hips my way. But no, as always she went down the hall to the bathroom.

As soon as she was gone, Nick disappeared into the other party rooms and came back with the rest of the guests trailing after him. He had a smirk on his face, a boner between his legs and the remote control in his hand.

He hit STOP and the porn bitch vanished. He hit a few more buttons and the whole screen—almost the entire wall—filled with Rory. She was leaning against the bathroom door with her catsuit unzipped all the way to her crotch, her tits spilling out.

"Boys and girls," Nick announced, undoing his fly. "This is live."

On the screen Rory squeezed her jugs—a porn move, a "somebody is watching" move, yet there was something different about the way she did it. I tilted my head, trying to identify what it was that was so unusual and then finally it came to me. Rory was neither looking into the camera nor avoiding it. She wasn't trying to show us her best angle or trying to arrange a sexy fuck face for our viewing pleasure. *This is totally genuine, totally unself-conscious,* I concluded, breaking into a wide grin. *She has no idea she's being filmed.*

Rory pressed her hand against her cunt and humped the whole thing—palm and fingers. *That's what dogs look like when they fuck,* I thought, and then I realized that without intending to, I'd also begun to diddle myself. But then I looked around the room and noticed that I wasn't alone. All of the guests at the party—about fifty men and women in total—had stopped screwing each other and now, with their eyes fixed to the screen, they were jerking themselves off.

Yes, Nick had come up with a scheme greater than I'd ever hoped for and certainly greater than I'd thought him capable of.

I loved how the men were milking their cocks—just yanking at them as if they were going to pull them off.

Rory plunged into her hole and then with her newly juicy finger she pressed ever smaller, harder circles into her clit. Her breathing went ragged and her hips stopped bucking until they were still like coils are still, still but with a contracted force behind them that's sure to explode—just a question of when. Nick, however, exploded first. He grunted, then his seed shot out and sprayed my thigh. *Fucker,* I would normally have thought, not wanting anything to do with his come. But I was so close myself I almost liked how it felt, dripping down my leg.

One guest after another followed Nick's lead—the exhibitionists screaming louder than porn bitches; the men squirting everywhere. I imagined their come spewing all over Rory—all over her catsuit and her exposed tits and her wriggling finger. And I buckled then, jerking hard against my own hand on my cunt, which was slick, swollen and feverishly hot. Rory's hand on Rory's cunt. My hand on Rory's. Rory's on mine. I saw all these combinations as I came, as Rory came.

Rory zipped up her catsuit and washed her hands with soap. Then she turned out the light and left the bathroom.

On his remote control, Nick pressed STOP and REWIND, making Rory's orgasm undo itself. We watched her jerk in reverse while (in real time) Rory's heels clicked down the hall, coming toward us. Then, just as she breezed into the room, Nick pressed PLAY.

4 | SLIP BACK IN TIME

Use Your Memories

Memory is more indelible than ink.
                              —Anita Loos

It was the best of times, it was the... No, forget the worst of times. Focus on the best. Was there one special moment that worked for you? One particular place you played in? One evening of arousal like none other? One event that rocked you all night long? It doesn't matter if you're not in Paris now, or if you've long lost the dress you were wearing, or if the movie theater where the two of you had hot balcony sex has been transformed into a Borders bookstore. Recreating a special moment doesn't mean reliving each step exactly. You'll bring something new to the occasion every time. But putting yourself into the past can enhance the pleasure you feel now.

Reliving a favorite time can be a serious turn-on, especially if you are able to build on what you started with. Wish you'd gotten busy under the bleachers after the big game? Well, put down your pompoms, it looks to me as if the quarterback's about to score, as happens in "The Big Touchdown" by Erica Dumas, where a couple reenacts a situation from years before:

"You looked so good running through those routines," you say as my head bobs up and down in your lap. "I couldn't wait to get you alone after the game. Why do you think I ran so fast?"

My mouth slides off you and I beam up at you. "You're just saying that!"

"No, really." Your voice is hoarse. "If your ass hadn't looked so fine every time that skirt flew up, I wouldn't have been able to run like that. I couldn't wait to get a piece of it."

I giggle and slide your cock between my lips again, feeling my pussy surge with every downward thrust. You're moaning again, a little louder, getting more excited as my hand works the shaft of your cock and my tongue circles the head. Your hands find the back of my cheerleader jersey and unzip it, pulling it forward. I ease my arms out so you can reach down to stroke my breasts through my sports bra. When you pull it up, I moan louder. Your fingers stroke my nipples through the damp material. You're getting closer, your arousal mounting as I bring you nearer your orgasm with every swirl of my tongue.

You pull me off of your cock, both of us panting.

"Kristi, please, just let me put it in a little," you beg.

I blush deeply. "Mi-i-ike!" I say, drawing your name out into three syllables.

"Please. I promise I won't come. I promise I'll go slow."

Memories can also serve to get you in the mood before the two of you get together. In "Field of (Day)Dreams" by Casey

Ferguson, the memories tug at the character, in a bittersweet way most people will relate to:

They stopped, just past the creek; pulled over on the shoulder, and ran laughing down the hill, ratty blanket from the trunk flapping out behind them.

She remembers how tall the weeds were, how they sank down in them like they were drowning, clutching at each other. She remembers how his kisses swallowed her moans, the sensation of his thumbs dragging across her nipples, his hands shoved under her shirt. There was frantic unlacing, wriggling free of clothing, sliding against each other, the pleasurable shock of wind against her naked body.

She remembers the hum of insects, the far off chatter of happy families by the creek, remembers the feel of grasses beneath her naked shoulder.

It was so warm; the air heavy with water, every inch of their bodies slick with sweat, glowing with heat. At the time, she noticed mostly the muscles of his shoulders, jumping under her hands; his prick, slick and hard against her legs; his lips pulling at her nipples, his breath blowing cool against her heated skin. They fucked for hours—in her memory, anyway...

But how do you make the most of your memories, when the past can be so fleeting? Draw up a list of the times that blew you away, your most spectacular orgasms, the sweetest kisses you ever shared. Then swap lists with your lover and see if you have any overlap. Who knows? Most likely you'll be making some brand-new memories very soon.

LE PETIT DÉJEUNER

Jeremy Edwards

A s much as we enjoy getting it on at night, it is the morning that is our special time. Nighttime sex is torrid and wild. When our evening draws to an end and Lisa lands sprawling on the bed, I sometimes think her panties will evaporate into thin air from the sheer heat of her cunt.

At night, we are fuckers.

In the morning, our passion is quiet, beautiful, and intense. We are lovers.

We fell in love in Paris. Our first kiss was in front of the Eiffel Tower. Perhaps this is why we've done our best to make the apartment resemble a little corner of France, within the great city of Cleveland, Ohio. When no one is listening, we refer to the immediate neighborhood as the *arrondissement*. The bookshelves are sprinkled with Balzac and *Asterix*. Unassuming Rhône wines haunt the kitchen counter, echoing the mood of the lazy still life that freshens the living room with flowers and peaches.

The bed we share sports continental linens, which we launder in lavender-scented detergent. The coffee whose aroma permeates our morning atmosphere is, *bien sûr,* a French Roast. Amazingly, there is an authentic *patisserie* within walking distance, and I venture there for croissants each day while Lisa bathes. As I return with the croissants she emerges, smelling like olive-oil soap in particular and delicious little French hotels in general. If there should happen to be a dusting of Great Lakes snow on the topmost pastry, I choose to imagine that it transubstantiates into confectioner's sugar as soon as the croissants and I enter Lisa's warm sphere of influence.

We always awake hungry for each other, but also just plain hungry. We breakfast from a rustic Provençal tray—at which true Parisian sophisticates would turn up their noses, but whose sunny yellow cheers us on winter days. Keeping the flaky crumbs out of the linens has long since been declared, by mutual assent, a lost cause. By now, I boast a prodigious adroitness with our handheld vacuum cleaner.

After croissants and coffee, our flesh mingles among the crisp linens. The scents of our bodies bond with the coffee and bakery aromas. I start by stroking Lisa's ass. It is firm and tastefully lewd like the peaches in the still life. She coos and wiggles, communicating the desire for my caresses. I, of course, fulfill this desire *tout de suite.* I alternate between pleasuring her ass and petting her hair, her back, and her thighs, watching her tremble as she enjoys anticipating my return to her bottom. She folds her arms between her head and the pillow, relishing the passivity of being touched, and letting her ecstasy express itself through her legs only. Her muscular limbs kick with exuberant bliss; they squeeze together and release, and her toes curl and flex.

When I venture between Lisa's thighs, I feel as if I'm having dessert. Dessert with breakfast, luxury of luxuries! And when I coax her nectar down, it tastes as sweet to me as marmalade. She takes hold of my *baguette*, where a drop of *crème* has already appeared.

Where her cunt tastes like sweets, her mouth tastes like love. I want to lick and taste every inch of her, not in the raunchy way I devour her at night, but slowly, sweetly. I cup the satisfying roundness of her *derrière*, a perfect bowl, in fact, of sensuality.

And yet, no bowl bounds my conception of Lisa. She is a horizonless landscape of delicious, sustaining beauty, from the buttery freshness of her neck to the sensitive nook under each arm to the shiny daintiness of her toenails. I want to frolic atop her, squirm into her, come over her. She is a picnic in the park and the softball game afterward, a dip in the lake and a roll in the mud...the summer day that only wanes so that it may enchant you again as a summer evening. I want to be totally embraced by her love, her acceptance, her cunt, her smile. I want to pet, tickle, squeeze, lick and ride her till our nerves melt together into soup. I want to see her lips mouth "I love you" when she can no longer speak.

As we make love, I imagine that we are back in Paris. That there is a bidet in our bathroom. That people are speaking French on the sidewalk below. That around the corner is the little pharmacy where I had to resort to an earthy pantomime to indicate that I required a box of condoms, and where the pharmacist, a handsome woman of about thirty-five with dark, humorous eyes, smiled knowingly at me when I paid for them.

"Tell me about the *pharmacienne*," Lisa requested our last night in Paris, just as I was penetrating her with bedtime vigor. "Fuck me and tell me how she looked at you." Lisa got off on the idea that the druggist had watched me as if she wanted to personally administer the dose of condoms she had provided. Lisa still asks to hear about it some nights, three years later.

On other nights, she wants to know all about the pretty Swiss tourist across the aisle on the bus, the one that I'd noticed, out of the corner of my eye, subtly stroking her skirt while she adored a Degas nude in a gallery at the Musée d'Orsay. Lisa likes to have me relate how this art lover delicately, but deliberately, flashed her blonde sex at me as our bus bumped along the boulevard, her smirking gaze fixed on my face. As we slide together on the midnight mattress, I talk to Lisa in broken, abrupt sentences about the tourist who winked at me with her cunt.

But I digress.

The French Roast has heightened all my sensitivities. My cock strives for Lisa's body, and my cerebral synapses fire like good old American popcorn at the erotic implications of her every sensuous motion. In the faux-French Cleveland morning, the walls of Lisa's pussy absorb each of my strokes so tenderly, yet with such solidity, I feel totally supported by her intimate embrace, just as I feel completely supported by Lisa in every aspect of our life. Her cunt understands my cock the way her mind understands my own, and her emotions respond with such sensitivity to my innermost needs. Pulsating inside her, I feel her so tangibly as the source of all my small and large joys.

We fell in love in Paris, but I had only an inkling of what I was falling in love with. I fell in love with her laughter and came to know her kindness. I fell in love with her acuteness and came to know her wisdom. I fell in love with her sexy ass and came to know the ineffable rapture of being clasped every morning in her transcendent feminine grip.

Ask me to describe Lisa's face, and I cannot find the words. I can no longer see her features discretely as eyes, mouth, nose, chin...all I see is the light, the personality, the embodiment of a compassionate intelligence that is my sun and my soil. I can describe Lisa no better than I can describe the sensation of water quenching my thirst, or the flavor of fresh air in my lungs. I might as well try to describe what it feels like to be a living being.

In Paris, she was pretty as a picture. Now, I rarely see her in two dimensions. Still, there are those moments when I walk into the bedroom and observe a gorgeous creature splayed for me, waiting to be touched, waiting to have her oils made to flow, waiting to absorb me and acquire me once again...and I frame Lisa in my mind like a luscious painting; a canvas, magically enough, that I can step inside.

Orgasm is inextricably associated with the aromas of coffee and pastry and lavender. In the morning, we always come slowly, writhing in down-tempo sensuality, savoring our shuddering moments together.

We are lovers. We are lovers. We are lovers this morning.

5 | SLEEP ON IT

Devour Your Dirty Dreams

We fucked—fast, urgent, silent.
Your skin was gold and slippery.
Afterward we waltzed through empty streets.
The world was asleep,
and we were dreaming in color.
—Nikki Magennis, "Madrid"

Everyone has wet dreams. Not everyone remembers them. But if you are one of the lucky few who can stretch out in the still-warm sheets and remember your dirty dreams, why not confess these uninhibited fantasies to your partner? Who knows, he or she might just make your dreams come true. As Cinderella sang, "A Dream Is a Wish Your Heart Makes." (Although she probably wasn't talking about the types of dreams I'm discussing here!)

But dreams-come-true is what we're after here. Like the woman in "Canvas" by Renee Roberts, who confesses her dreams of her lover covering her with tattooed designs:

I dream of her inking me, of her using a silver-tipped needle to draw along the lines of my back, to turn me into a work of art. I envision the designs that would cover my skin, the clichéd images: a heart with a scroll that says her name; a dragon whose wings would beat whenever I flexed my muscles; a snake with rippling, iridescent scales on its belly.

And then she wakes to discover that her dreams have been brought to reality:

In the morning, when the sun wakes me up, she's gone. I roll onto my side, slowly, achingly. I stand and make my way to the bathroom. I've peed, blown my nose, splashed water on my face, before I look in the bathroom mirror. Before I see the black markings she's penned on me, all over me, the visions, the dreamlike images she's drawn while I slept.

Sometimes, sex right on the cusp of dreaming can be transcendent, as Marie Potoczny shows in "The Other Side of Sleep":

"I know you're awake," he says.

I smile; I can't help but smile and then feign sleep, snore prettily, slightly tipsy, but tilt my hips for him to curl behind me. He reaches his other hand around in front of me, in between my legs, and I scissor them wide for him, wide for me.

"Don't wake me, I'm sleep groping," he whispers in my ear. "Never wake a sleep groper."

I laugh. Sleep laugh.

He pushes inside me and I hold my body still for him to find the hard bottom of penetration.

"Ah," he says.

"Ah," I say.

The lovers in "Arran's Lure" by Saskia Walker choose sex over sleep:

They barely slept, afraid to waste the precious time together. Instead they had fucked hard then made love slow. They'd lain awake in the moonlight communicating with mouths, fingers, and tongues. They explored each other almost continually, talking endlessly, then rolling together, his mouth on her pussy, hers on his cock, devouring each other.

Then there's the deliriously sexy sensation of being in a waking dream, like this scene from "Pervertable" by Mathilde Madden:

Your voice was so dark and honeyed, it seemed to make my spine vibrate. "No, don't go easy on me," I said softly, almost as if I were in a dream, in one of my fantasies. "No, I like pain."

You gave a dark chuckle. "We'll see, I'll give you twenty and see how you go."

And the heat of your body was gone, suddenly, and your sweet smell became more and more distant. Panting hard, I waited.

Reality can be even sexier than fiction (which is, truly, the point of this whole book). Most of the readers I know swooned over Sommer Marsden's fact-based story "Get Into My Head":

My husband is a very low-key guy. The reason we are still married after thirteen years together is that he still knows how to really get into my head. Like last night. We're sitting on the sofa and he asked me to do something. I said, "Nah! You do it. I am comfy." Very softly he said, "You are such a brat." That made me pause. All those baby hairs on the back of my neck went up and I just sat there. Quietly. That is an act of God. Me being quiet.

"See, you are a brat. That's why maybe you need a spanking. Like the one I dreamed about last night."

Dead. Silence. From me.

"We were in public, too. You had done something. You had that Sommer tone. And I pulled you over my leg and for whatever reason you were completely naked from the waist down. And I bent down and said in your ear, 'Everyone can see you.

*You know that, right? Do you care?' And you said 'Yes.' And
you said 'No.' You said whatever I wanted, so I wouldn't stop.
Or maybe so I would stop. I don't know."*

*He shrugged. "Then I woke up. Maybe we'll see what
happens tonight."*

*Whew. And that is what preoccupies me all through today
as I attempt to do all the things I need to do. In my brain, I am
being spanked in public. And I'm still waiting to find out what
happens.*

Sex dreams can be twisted in the most delicious ways. Just
look what happened when I opened up my blog to dreamers:

*I dreamed I was the tall blonde Viennese whore described by
Henry Rollins in* Black Coffee Blues. *I was in red shiny vinyl and
mile-high lace-up stripper boots. It was cold out, but I wasn't.
I didn't need sleep or food or love. Just cock and cash. Between
tricks I stood up against the side of an ancient brick building
and stared ahead, expressionless, hard—all business. That was a
good dirty dream.—KM*

*I don't know who he was...but I was outside on a balcony over-
looking a city. I was wearing a tight white T-shirt and a pair of
sheer black knickers. It was raining and my hair was plastered
to my head and down the back of my shirt. He came up behind
me and grabbed me by the hair and said something to the effect
of what a dirty girl I was, letting people watch. He pushed my
panties aside, made me hold on to the balcony, and drove into
me over and over while he kissed and bit my neck, played with
my breasts through the wet shirt and finally, finally touched me
through the front of my knickers.—Kelly*

I had a beautiful dream about a guy I was seeing when I was younger, he had long blond hair and a goatee, very Metallica; he was gorgeous. And I dreamt he was standing in my conservatory; it had been raining, and he and the glass were covered in tiny sparkling raindrops, the light shining prisms through them. It was beautiful.—Jo

Most of my intense dreams involve one of my best friends from college. I do also have some dreams about sex with my amazing husband, but it's different than the sex we generally have—a bit more kink—often silk is involved.—Kiki

My own dreams tend to cling to me. I wake up and make coffee. I take a run, then a shower. But the sexy dreams cover me, so thin the fibers are nearly transparent. When I stand in the bathroom and look at my reflection, I still see the dream draped over me.

There's no telling where your dreams will take you.

THE PRINCESS AND THE PENIS

Ronald Keller

S lanted shafts of light streamed through the open curtains, bathing the king-sized bed in warm sunlight. Sprawled out in the light with the covers tossed to one side, Princess slumbered, the bright shafts turning her filmy silk nightshirt into a translucent veil, shrouding her tempting curves. It was 8:00 a.m. on a Sunday, the morning after our first date. We had made love late into the morning, and now Princess lay exhausted.

Her real name was Carolyn, but I preferred to think of her by the name she used to post on the Sleepy Girls website: Princess.

I nuzzled up against her, remembering the tender moments we'd shared the night before. My cock started to harden.

Princess and I had chatted online for months before discovering that we lived in the same city. By then, Princess had confessed all her fondest erotic dreams, and they had one thing in common.

My favorite fantasy is to be made love to while sleeping,

she'd told me in an email early on in our interaction. *And not to be awakened.*

I'm a very deep sleeper, she'd added. *But no one's ever been able to do it.*

I nudged my lips up against her ear and whispered softly, "Princess?"

She sighed gently in her slumber. Her eyes flickered suggestively under their lids. I wondered what she was dreaming.

She lay on her back. Her breasts strained through the thin material of her nightie, her nipples erect. Whatever she was dreaming, I was quite sure it was interesting.

I ran my fingertips over her breasts and down, caressing the curve of her thighs and touching her pussy through her filmy string panties. I moved slowly, careful not to upset the bed. I tugged her panties down over her smooth ass, drawing them away from her pussy, still moist from last night's reverie. I eased her panties down her thighs, over her calves. I slipped them over her ankles and tossed them away.

"Princess?" I whispered.

She didn't make a move. She really was a very deep sleeper.

I eased her legs open and slid, naked, on top of her. I began to nuzzle her ear, whispering, "This is for you," as I nudged the entrance of her pussy with the head of my cock. It was slick with arousal and opened wide for my cock. She gasped as the head entered her; I paused as her mouth worked in somnambulant mumbles and then her eyes went back to rolling in their REM-sleep dance. With a slow thrust, I entered her all the way, and a tiny, sleepy sigh escaped her lips.

Her pussy embraced me, wet and tender. I started to slide gently in and out of her, my hands gently caressing her breasts through silk. She moaned in her sleep, but didn't say a word. I entered her rhythmically in slow, savoring thrusts, loving the way her pussy reacted to me while her eyes continued their midnight fandango. I kissed her slightly parted lips; they remained slack, loose, motionless.

A tiny whimper rumbled through her throat, as her hips began to pulse in response to my thrusts. I said her name again.

"Princess?"

She lay still and did not respond.

With a few more thrusts, however, her hips began to grind, her body taking over while her mind was disengaged. She started to thrash in her sleep, clawing the bed as she writhed under me. I was almost on the edge of my own orgasm when I realized Princess was going to come.

I can have orgasms in my sleep, she'd told me in an early email. *I guess they're like wet dreams.*

This dream was definitely wet—soaking. Her pussy, tight around my cock, was moistening further as her sleeping body strove toward orgasm. When she began to shudder, I felt the spasms of her pussy around my cock, gripping me in a tender embrace as she came. Her lips parted wide and her breath came out in a rapturous moan. All the while, her eyes continued to move.

I came, my cock seized by the ecstasy of her pussy's embrace. I moaned and kissed her sleeping lips, not even caring anymore if I awakened her. But she remained still, now, sleeping. Her eyes had paused in their movements.

I lay atop her and sank back into exhaustion, loving the feel of her body curled against me.

It was after noon when she awakened again, stretching in the slanted sunlight, her perfect body moist with the sweat of sleep.

"Oh, I had the most beautiful dream," she sighed. Her eyes opened sleepily and she smiled.

"Please tell me it was true," she whispered.

"Every minute of it," I said, and kissed her.

6 | DROP ME A LINE

Pen a Lusty Letter

To write a good love letter, you ought to begin without knowing what you mean to say, and to finish without knowing what you have written.
— Jean-Jacques Rousseau

Love letters are sweet. Press them between pages of a dictionary and keep them forever. But *lust* letters? The sort of filth-o-grams to make your pulse pound? Even better. Lewd, lascivious, filled with the decadent details of what a faraway lover (or a close-by lover) would like to do to you, or have you do in return—these are truly the letters to cherish. If you haven't saved any of these, write some brand-new ones. Slide one in the side bag on her Harley. Slip one into the pocket of his chaps. (Oh, wait. Do chaps have pockets?)

> Then you walked up to me and gave me the
> most sensual, warm, wet kiss. I had to pull
> away at first, but it was to incredible so I
> reached for you, still sitting on the couch, and
> gave you one.
>   Now I didn't care who the hell was watching.

Don't stifle yourself. With pen in hand, pour out your fantasies:

I want you to bend me over, pull down my panties and spank me with your hand.

Or:

I want you to drop to your knees, unbutton my 501s and suck me off.

Write down exactly what you'd like to happen to you. Shanna Germain describes the type of note she wants her lover to write to her in "How to Spank Me: An Open Letter to My Future Lovers":

First, leave a note on the bed before you leave for work, telling me what to wear. I'll find it on your pillow when I wake up, and smile when I realize you've chosen the pleated pink miniskirt, a white baby-doll T-shirt and those bottom-hugging white panties that you bought me for my birthday, three to a package. Suggest, in your carefully crafted scrawl, that I wear heels. I'll know that you mean my three-inch-high strappy black sandals, the ones that let you see my toes. In your PS, tell me that you'll be home at 3:00, and that I'd better be ready.

If you're feeling particularly kinky, write to your lover's favorite body part. This is what my character Jo does in "To Lola, With Love": she writes to her girlfriend's pussy.

I'm not exactly sure how to admit this—it sounds funny to

say, and looks funnier on paper—but my girlfriend is having an affair with my vagina. She'll readily admit to it. She's even written love letters to it. Yes, indeed; Jo, my normally sane, very lovely dyke sweetheart has taken pen in hand and written to my cunt.

Think about what part of your lover makes your body hum with pleasure. Then pick up a pen and write a note. Short is fine. Simple is right on. Even Post-it notes stuck on a coffee cup in the morning, or letters written in lipstick on the bathroom mirror count as love letters. Your goal? To let your partner know how turned on he or she makes you feel.

Lust covers a lot of territory, from barely risqué to truly deviant, and your letters can vary just as widely. Length is unimportant: one day you might write only a line. Another day you might find yourself writing several pages in a single sitting.

My man sometimes adds sexy items to the grocery list. He knows I won't see the words until I am in the middle of the produce section, or back by the freezer. Then suddenly, the items jump out at me, in between *eggs* and *bread* might be *fuck me senseless*. Needless to say, I try not to buy too many perishables on those trips. God knows the groceries are going to sit on the counter for a while before we wind up unpacking them.

If you have a difficult time coming up with ideas, do a little research. Try reading the white-hot letters in *Penthouse Variations* or *Forum*. Or peruse some dirty poetry from the likes of Leonard Cohen, Baudelaire, Michael Madsen or Shakespeare. And remember, even the *act* of writing a letter can be a turn-on; just check out "Taking Dictation" by N. T. Morley:

With a shudder, Mr. Williams drives his cock into Miss White's pussy, eliciting from her full, lipsticked lips a squeal remarkably like the one Mr. Williams just finished describing. Miss White wriggles her ass back and forth, snuggling her cunt down onto

Mr. Williams' shaft as he begins to pound her. Her shorthand is becoming quite illegible, but she continues to scrawl as Mr. Williams dictates.

"From the way you pumped back onto my cock, though," grunted Mr. Williams in time with his thrusts into Miss White, *"I knew right away that you wanted it as bad as I did. I fucked you good, Kymberlee, and you gave as good as you got. I fully intended to take that snug little back door of yours, Kymberlee, but you were even more eager than I was. You looked over your shoulder and begged me to fuck you in the ass. 'Ram it in my butthole,' I think, were your exact words, 'make me your little fucking ass-bitch.' Excellent choice of words, Kymberlee, reinforcing my confidence that your oral skills were more than adequate for the tasks of this job. Do you like to get fucked in the ass, Miss White? Miss White, you're not transcribing."*

Miss White is sprawled across the desk, moaning uncontrollably, a puddle of drool having formed under her red-painted lips on the glistening surface of the polished oak desk. Her ass is lifted high to receive the thrusts of Mr. Williams' cock, and her eyes are shut tight as she shudders in bliss.

Taking dictation has never been quite so deliriously sexy, nor has writing a business letter. See? It's all in how you perform even the most mundane tasks.

EROTIC FICTION

BEFORE
SLEEP DOES

Sommer Marsden

D ear Sir,

I couldn't stop thinking about you. Somehow what we did the other night got into my head and wouldn't leave. Seems like forever since we were together, but it's only been two days! And five more days until you come back and we can pick up where we left off. I'm really tired and it's very hot and part of me thinks that if I write all of the things in my head down on paper, I will be able to crawl under our white cotton sheet and go to sleep. Once the words are out of me, I can turn the fans on high and drift off to the summer night sounds. Here goes...

You'll notice that I addressed this to Sir. It's one of the things I've never admitted to you—the secret desire that you'll make me call you Sir. Make me submissive to you. I've daydreamed of your telling me how bad I am when I fail to do as I'm told. I imagine it would be really hard to remember to call you Sir when I have never done it before. And every time you address me (in this fantasy), I blunder and forget to address you with respect, forget to call you by the title you have specified. You get so angry with me. I feel my face heat up with a hot shameful blush and I can't seem to stand still. I have to shift and move just the tiniest bit in the small plaid skirt you have dressed me in. My knee-highs seem too hot and my heels too high and my stomach bottoms out because I know that I'm in trouble.

"Come over here," you say to me and I can barely move. I've never felt that trepidation with you before. But I do and part of me likes it. Likes it so very much that the crotch of my little white ruffled panties grows wetter and wetter with each second that ticks past. "Now. Not when you feel like it. Come over here now."

Somehow I manage to walk over. My knees feel like they're knocking but when I look I see that they aren't. It's just this new and intense anxiety mixed with excitement that has crossed all my wires and made me feel chaotic inside and so very horny on the outside. When you point to your lap, my pussy flickers and I feel the tiny blips of pleasure all through my body. They mix with the fear nicely. I've never been so hesitant and eager all at once.

Your lap, which is a familiar place, seems completely foreign as I drape myself over your knees and wait. It's hard to swallow and it's hard to breathe. I study my long blonde hair brushing the thick blue carpeting. When you lift my skirt, the difference in air temperature is so apparent. My bottom grows cool and when I think that in an instant you will warm it up, I shiver.

You don't give me warning. Not even a grunt or a laugh or a sigh. Your hand lands with a hearty smack and my head snaps back as fire floods my skin and moisture escapes me. "I think you need to count them off so you learn your lesson."

"One, Sir." Before I can finish saying "Sir," the second blow has landed and I'm squirming. Two, three and four leave me panting like a dog, with my head hanging down and my ass sticking up. I'm not really sure how many you are going to give me and I'm terrified to ask. I don't know if I'm more scared of there being a lot more or the idea that you might almost be done.

"I bet," you say more to yourself than to me, "I just bet I know what I'll find." I start to shake when your fingers explore the outside of my panties. You trace the seam of my pussy with your finger and I know you can feel the wetness there as surely as I can. You stay silent as you swoop the pad of your finger up and down that cloth-covered slit until I am biting my tongue to keep from begging and clenching my thighs to keep from squirming. My cunt has picked up the tempo of my heartbeat, and it's a greedy, fast rhythm.

Right then and there, I feel like I will die if you don't put some part of yourself in me: your finger, your tongue, your cock, anything. I want to be filled by you in some fashion and I'm terrified to ask and terrified not to. Instead I bow my head and say so softly, "Please."

Your fingers push aside the barrier of my panties and shove into me; two at first and when I hold my breath and then blow it out like I'm drowning, you add a third. I wiggle on them, at your beautiful mercy as you fuck me with your fingers. You know me so well; you keep me right on that edge, walking that tightrope until I think I might die.

Your fingers pull free and I don't even have time to protest before your hand lands with a fiery *crack!* and I buck under you as if I've been shocked. "Five, Sir," I cry and six follows so swiftly I add, "And six, Sir, six."

"You're so bad," you say to me and I love it. Secretly I love it. I know I am supposed to act ashamed and I do. And part of me is a bit ashamed for how much this is making me want you. It's crazy even to me how much I want to fuck you, but I love it too. In fact, I love it more than I could ever have imagined.

"I did not give you permission to get wet. I did not say you could get turned on. I think the only thing to do is make sure you really learn your lesson." My breath freezes and my heart skips in my chest. Your voice is full of menace and that makes me break out in goose bumps. You peel my silly little panties down so slowly I can count my heartbeats. Twenty-two heartbeats it takes for you to pull them to the middle of my thighs. They bind me there. I cannot spread my legs, I cannot move much at all. You smooth your big hand over my blazing hot ass and it feels so good. I can't help it. I arch up into your palm. Begging you not to stop but begging you to fuck me, too.

"Take my cock out." I do as I'm told and wait. I know I'm supposed to wait but I don't want to. I am holding your hard cock in my hand and waiting for you to tell me what to do next. "Suck me," you say and I almost say "Thank you," but I catch myself. I take you all the way in, all the hot length of you. I can smell our laundry detergent and your cologne and the distinct smell that is just you.

"Wait," you say. I pause and you deliver the next blow. I must focus not to tighten my mouth and teeth too much or I will bite and if I bite, I'm sure I will pay. "Keep going," you say and I do. But then you laugh. "You didn't say, 'Seven, Sir,' now did you?"

My face grows so hot and I shake my head. A single tear escapes and I clench my thighs and arch my back. Nothing relieves the crazy want and need buzzing under my skin. I just want you to fuck me now. I want to be done with the spanking and get to the fucking. But when you deliver the next harsh blow and the pain sings along my skin and makes my cunt flutter wildly with a pleasure that is nothing but pure potential, I am okay where I am. Okay but still wise enough to say, "Eight, Sir."

"We were to go to ten but I think eleven for the one you missed," you whisper and for just an instant, your fingers are back inside of me, striking that deep place that makes my pussy grow tight and then tighter still.

My body overrides my mind on nine, ten and eleven. I have your cock in my mouth and your hand on my ass. Pain is skimming along my skin so swiftly I feel dizzy. At the heart of it all is my cunt, wet and ready and just begging for you. So I beg, or my version of begging, finally laying my head in your lap. "Please," I say. That's it. Please.

You take pity on me, folding me over the seat of the chair before moving behind me. You slip your fingers back inside to test me and I'm so, so wet. "Slut," you laugh and I push back against you wantonly to confirm that it's true. I am a slut for you.

Your cock is impossibly hard and impossibly warm and you slide into me so slowly I think I might scream. I bite my lip instead and focus on patience. It's hard to focus because the friction of your entry has me already on the verge of coming. But that all fades away when you start to move and you are fucking me; blissfully, roughly, fucking me. You yank at my hips and thrust deeper. I can hear my hair whispering over the caned seat of the chair. "Oh, Sir, please," I say again.

You deliver one blow after another to my sore and heated ass. You fuck me harder, spank me harder, and when I come, I'm crying and calling your name. You come with me, which secretly pleases me. I love when we come together.

And that is why I addressed my letter to Sir. I want to call you Sir. For now, though, I will tuck this letter under your pillow until you come home. I hope you find it right away. Until then, I'll think about how it felt the last time you fucked me. And I'll relive this letter in my mind over and over. I know I'll have to touch myself before sleep will come. I will have to come before sleep does. That's fine with me. I'll detail it in full in my next letter. I have a few more days and there's a lot of room under your pillow.

All my love...

7 | BAT YOUR EYES

Be a Flirt

The amount of women in London who flirt with their own husbands is perfectly scandalous. It looks so bad. It is simply washing one's clean linen in public.

—Oscar Wilde

Flirt. What's that? You thought this was a guide to keeping the heat in a monogamous relationship. Oh, but it is. I mean flirt with each other. There is something so shivery and sexy about flirting, like the lovers do in "Hungry for Love" by Saskia Walker, where flirting is the foreplay over dinner:

We flirt across the restaurant table and our food, while I sit there thinking about what we're going to do when we're finally alone. It's a favorite pastime of mine, but you know that, don't you? And you love every minute of it because it gets me so wet. In fact, you'll find out just how wet it's getting me when you touch me there, later.

When was the last time you made eyes at your partner? The last time you did that look, look back, look away dance that is an international turn-on? Can't remember? Then too much time has gone by.

In "Choice of Toppings," Jeremy Edwards describes the thrill of desire: *Jill and I had been flirting for weeks. She had kind eyes and an endearing mop of strawberry-blonde hair, and she could keep up with me, quip for quip, where banter was concerned.*

Flirting lets people know that they're sexy. And, as Hugh Hefner said in a recent *Esquire* interview, "Everybody, if they've got their head on straight, wants to be a sexual object, among other things. They want to be attractive. Otherwise, what a sad and pathetic life. To really live a worthwhile life is to be attracted to and attractive to other people."

That's the job of flirting. To let someone know that you find him or her attractive. More than that, to let your partner know how much you want him. Rachel Kramer Bussel elaborates in "Check, Mate":

I picture a leisurely dance of flirtation, the kind whose power builds the longer it's made to wait, until we rip each other's clothes off and have at it.

This is the difficult part: stretching out that dance of flirtation, letting the exchange build up between the two of you; waiting as long as possible to get to the "rip each other's clothes off" stage, like in "A Taste of Italy" by Sommer Marsden:

He set his wineglass down and took her hand in his. He gave her palm small circular strokes with his thumb. The strokes might as well have been on her pussy for the results it provoked. A pulse started in her clit as arousal turned to urge. Her skimpy thong was suddenly sodden.

One of my favorite flirtation exchanges appears in Rachel Kramer Bussel's "Flirting with Santa":

I look up and meet his eyes straight on and feel a flush of pleasure run through me, the likes of which I rarely, if ever, feel at work. I'm the first to look away—I have to be, or else I may spill my drink down the front of my dress. I go seek out my comrade-in-office-arms, Cathy, and see if she knows who Santa is. "I don't know, but I know why you're asking," she teases. She's aware of most of my sexual peccadilloes and loves to tease me from the safety of her warm and cozy marriage, but I know she still gets a thrill out of my stories and adventures.

I try to kill time, making the obligatory rounds, tasting all the sweet offerings being passed around, until I can stand it no longer. I inch closer toward Santa, checking out not so much the outfit, which I'm already quite familiar with—padded red velvet suit trimmed in white, fluffy beard, jaunty hat—but the body underneath it. The way he is sitting—calm and almost expectant, with perhaps a twinkle in his eye—sends goose bumps up and down my body.

Normally I'd be getting ready to go at about this time, having made the obligatory small talk and eaten my weight in baked goods, but tonight there's nothing I'd rather do than get to know Santa just a little bit better. I drain my glass triumphantly, holding it close to my lips to let every last drop of glistening liquid slide into my mouth, knowing for sure that he is watching. My tongue darts out to lick the edges of the glass, treating the champagne as if it were cotton candy, savoring every little bit, and getting my tongue ready for action.

Flirting doesn't have to end in fucking. It doesn't have to be the start of foreplay. Flirt with your partner all the time: In line at the grocery store. On the phone. At the dry cleaner's. Once you start, you'll find flirting with each other is addictive and difficult to stop. But, really, who wants to stop?

THE RULES OF
THE GAME

Thomas S. Roche

I see you across the lobby, and you look incredible. You're wearing a little electric-blue dress that I've never seen you wear before—it's so tight and short and low cut that you look like a high-class call girl. The black bolero jacket doesn't diminish that impression—it's equally tight, accenting the swell of your full breasts in the snug, low-cut dress. You make such a fetching hooker that I almost guess the rules of the game, but you keep me duped for another few moments as I watch you sauntering toward me, a knowing smile on your full, red-painted lips. You've got a little string of pearls on, not to mention a pair of black sheer stockings and high-heeled shoes.

I understand—or, rather, I think I understand—why you asked me here, dressed up in an Armani suit and carrying a roll of hundred-dollar bills, to the lobby of the city's best hotel at 10:00 on a Tuesday night. A late dinner in the hotel restaurant—which has been getting rave reviews lately from the local papers—perhaps, and then a booty call in a hotel suite. The idea intrigues me, though I might have been just as happy to meet you in your apartment, where of late I've had the best sex of my life. Thinking about that, I can feel my cock stirring in my pants, already, before you even take the bar stool next to me.

"This seat taken?" you ask, once you're situated comfortably.

"No," I say, smiling. I'm about to say "Hi" and hug you, call you by your name. But before I can, you speak.

"I'm Simone," you tell me, putting out your hand for me to either shake it or kiss it. I'm taken aback at first: That's not your name at all. Not a middle name, nickname or alias—at least, not that I know of. Then it hits me—what you're doing, you naughty little thing.

"Pleased to meet you, ah, *Simone*," I tell you. I take your hand and kiss it. "I'm...Mike."

"Nice to meet *you, Mike*." Your lips curve around the word with contempt, telling me that you would know it was an alias even if we *hadn't* been sleeping together for months. "In town for the convention?"

I have to grope for the response, because it's just then that I've realized you're not wearing your usual scent—instead, it's something expensive but tawdry, suggestive and inviting.

"Yeah," I say nervously. "I'm in town for the convention." My head spins as I breathe in your scent, excited by the game you're playing. As you shift on the bar stool, I see your short dress riding up slightly, and I notice you've got garters attached to your lace-top stockings. I find myself wondering what else you're wearing under that tiny dress.

"What can I get you?" asks the bartender, a pert college-age girl wearing a white tuxedo shirt.

You look at me, raise your eyebrows.

"Can I buy you a drink?" I blurt nervously.

A charming, gracious smile crosses your face. "I'd love that. I'll have a cosmopolitan."

Of course you will, I think, and I order another Johnnie Walker Black, neat. You've never ordered a cosmopolitan since I've known you, but what else would a high-class whore order?

"I love the taste of scotch," you say. "It's so sexy on a man's lips."

I swallow nervously. This should be easy, smooth—after all, it's no surprise that you've seduced me into another erotic adventure. But I find my breath coming tight in my chest, my heart pounding as if you were really a stranger. Is it the scent? The clothes? Or the lascivious way you're looking at me, telling me that I'm nothing more than prey for you to run down, capture, and devour?

"Do you work around here?" I ask.

"You could say that," you say, smiling.

The bartender brings the drinks, and without missing a beat I pay for them and tip her with a five-dollar bill. She thanks me warmly and gives both of us a disapproving look—but her eyes linger longer on you, the whore of Babylon turning this expensive hotel into a two-bit bordello.

I drink half the scotch while you sip gingerly at your cosmo. "That's a very nice suit you're wearing," you tell me. "Your wife must help you shop."

I laugh uncomfortably, and only half of it is an act.

"Girlfriend?"

"Well," I say. "I've got a girlfriend."

"No kidding," you say, your lips toying with the cocktail straw. "I guess that's not a surprise with a guy like you. You know what they say."

"What do they say?" I gulp the rest of the scotch and

the bartender refills it without asking.

"All the good ones are taken. Your girlfriend's obviously a very lucky lady, Mike. Been together long?"

"Almost a year," I say. Then I smile. "She's great, but she could be a little more adventurous."

I see your eyes narrow, and I know that with that simple statement I've changed the rules of the game, hooking you with the promise of forbidden knowledge—however counterfeit—and reeling you in before you even know it.

But you remain cool, playing it to the hilt.

"Adventurous, Mike?"

"You know...in bed."

"Oh," you say, sipping at your drink. "*Sexually* adventurous."

"That's right," I say. "I hope I haven't shocked you."

You giggle, your lips pursing as you stare at me.

"Oh, no, Mike," you sigh. "I doubt anything you could say would shock me."

"Oh, that's a relief," I say.

"I mean, what is it your girlfriend doesn't want to do?" you ask me. "Whatever it is, I'm sure there's a girl out there who would be happy to oblige."

"You think? Just the other night, I wanted to hang from the chandeliers. And she said to me, 'But honey, what about the security deposit?'"

"Really."

I drink my scotch, smiling at you.

"Well, I'm sure all sexually potent men such as yourself have some things their wives or girlfriends won't do. For instance, it's a well-known fact that most men need a good hard spanking, isn't it?"

"Is it?"

"Yes," you say, pursing your lips. "A really good hard one.

Especially when they're being smart-asses, which certain men do with great regularity."

"Is that so?"

You smile and laugh. "Then again, if they're adventurous themselves, they should really be rewarded, don't you think? After all, some women really *like* it when a man wants naughty things. Chandeliers aside."

"Some women?"

"Uh-huh." Your tongue teases the cocktail straw, your eyes undressing me over the rim of the glass.

The bartender is frowning at us. "Another cosmo, ma'am?"

"Please," I say. "Allow me."

"Of course. Thank you." You smile at the bartender, and blow her a kiss. She reddens and looks away.

"So what naughty things do you *really* want, Mike? You aren't fooling me with that comment about the chandeliers. I bet there's something really dirty that you're just dying to try, isn't there?"

"Well," I say. "There isn't really anything...."

"Oh, come now. Something you wouldn't dare ask your wife? I mean girlfriend?"

"Girlfriend," I say.

"Something you think she'd never do?"

"Well," I say.

"Come on," you say. "I'm a total stranger. You can admit everything to me, and no one will ever know. And don't tell me it's something like oral sex—I'm sure your girlfriend knows how to provide on that count."

"Oh yes," I say quickly. "She's...she's incredible."

"Really," you smile. "She gives good head?"

I glance around surreptitiously, making sure no one can hear.

"In-fucking-credible," I say. "She gives the best head I've ever had."

You giggle. "You should never tell that to a woman you've just met, Mike. She might take it as a challenge."

"No kidding."

"Come on," you say teasingly. "You're changing the subject. True confessions time."

"You first."

"Oh, now it's about me?" You lean close to me on the bar stool. "You want to know what I fantasize about?"

"I'll show you mine if you show me yours."

Our eyes meet, and for an instant it's almost like I *don't* know you, like this complex game we're playing has opened up a new woman inside you.

"Are you faithful, Mike?"

"To my girlfriend?"

"Of course."

"Oh, absolutely," I say.

"Because that's what I fantasize about," you say softly, leaning even closer to make sure no one can hear. "Finding a man such as yourself, a really...good-looking, sexy man, successful..."

"Um, thanks," I say, reddening.

"A man who would never, ever think about cheating on his girlfriend; a man who's totally, completely trustworthy. And making him go mad with lust, so mad that he can't control himself, that he betrays his girlfriend without even thinking about it."

I stare into your eyes, my heart pounding.

"Don't you think that would be sexy, *Mike*?"

"I...I don't know."

"Don't you think it would be sexy to totally lose everything, lose all hope of being the man you want to be, and just totally give yourself over to some slut in a hotel room? Some woman you've never met before?"

Now I'm breathing hard, and when I down the last of my scotch the bartender doesn't refill it. She's over on the far end of the bar, polishing glasses and scowling at us.

"Yes," I say, leaning close and putting my hand in the small of your back. "I guess that would be sexy."

You sigh, pulling away and reaching back to gently push my hand away. "Of course, it's just a fantasy," you say, and tip your empty glass to the bartender. She doesn't look happy at all about getting you another drink, but she sets us both up and I toss a Jackson on the bar. She ignores it.

"Just a fantasy," you say sadly, your tongue toying with the rim of your glass.

"It doesn't have to be," I say.

You look into my eyes again, smile.

"It doesn't?"

"No," I say.

"But you just told me you were faithful. I assumed you were completely out of my league. I mean, you would never want to—"

"Please," I say. "Let's get a room."

You laugh. "Now, Mike…you're not going to tell me you're thinking of cheating on your girlfriend, are you? You just told me she gives you the best head you've ever had."

"She does," I say. "Incredible."

"You're going to risk all that for a few hours in a hotel room with a woman you don't even know? You must think I'll give you even better head."

My cock is so hard, now, I'm afraid I won't be able to walk to the front desk. "Please," I say. "I'll get a room. On me."

"Well, Mike…I'm afraid I've got to leave for the airport in just a few minutes. I couldn't possibly miss my flight."

"Please," I tell you. "Please stay. I'd love to get to know you better."

"I bet you would," you say, now leaning away from me and turning your shoulders so you're facing the bartender rather than me. She's begun to ignore us completely.

"Can't you change your flight?"

"I'm afraid it's nonrefundable."

You're so good, I could almost believe you really are a call girl. You've reeled me in, and a strong force within me believes that you're really ready to walk out the door leaving me panting with desire, unsatisfied and angry. It's so complicated, so intricate, I want to laugh. But I don't, because this game has gotten serious, and the throbbing of my cock in my pants is telling me that there's no chance, now, that either one of us is willing to lose.

"I'll pay for your flight," I say.

You turn back toward me, arching your back so your breasts stretch invitingly through the fabric of your little blue dress. I can see your erect nipples, and rather than telling me that you're as turned on as I am, that you're as vulnerable as me, what I see in them is my own inexorable lust, leading me into a manufactured Gehenna of sin and damnation. And I don't care. I just want you, want to wrap my lips around each of those firm nipples and taste them. Want to slide that little blue dress off of you and bear your body, naked, deep into the softness of these expensive hotel beds.

"Oh, I couldn't let you do that."

"I'll pay for your flight...and your hotel room."

"Now, Mike, surely you know that I'm not going to share a room with you—I barely know you."

"I'll get you another room." You're my girlfriend, but I'm so consumed by desire for you I wouldn't dream of reminding myself that I can have you any night at home. I want you here, now, upstairs in a rented room.

"Well," you say, leaning toward me again, your hand resting

in my lap, your fingertips brushing my cock. "We'll see about that. For now, maybe you should just get one."

"How much?"

"How much what, Mike?"

"How much is your flight?"

"Five hundred dollars," you say.

"Even?"

"Yes," you tell me. "Five hundred dollars even. Do you have the cash?"

"Yes," I say.

"You expected me."

"I'll get a room."

You lean closer, your breath sweet in my face. "All right. Bring me back the key and leave the cash by the door when you go in the room. I'll meet you up there in a few minutes."

"Don't go anywhere," I tell you.

"Oh, Mike," you say softly, your lips just barely brushing mine. "I wouldn't dream of it."

I know it's all a game; I made love to you just last night, to our overwhelming mutual satisfaction. But I feel like I've stumbled into your darkest fantasy, the edge you walk when you're feeling really bad. And you're good at it—better than I could have dreamed. The strange thing is, I don't care. I don't care that it's all artifice, that we're lovers and you're as far from being a call girl as a woman can be. I don't care at all—I just care that I have to have you, right now, in a hotel room, calling you "Simone" and paying you five hundred dollars to fuck me.

When I return to the bar, you're sitting there chatting with the bartender, who seems to have become more friendly since I left. The two of you are laughing together like old friends.

I come over to your bar stool, take your hand, press the key into it. I lean forward to kiss you, but you turn your face and receive my kiss on your cheek.

Your act is impressive—no money's changed hands, so I don't get a thing. I smile at you, my cock hard in my pants.

"See you upstairs?" I whisper.

"Yes, darling," you say. "I'll just be a few minutes." You wink at the bartender, who blushes.

When I open the door, I'm greeted by that familiar smell of a clean hotel room. I shut the door behind me and turn on the light next to the king-sized bed. I angle it toward the wall—mood lighting.

I'm not sure what to do next—do I greet you with a drink in my hand? Do I take you in my arms as you walk in the door? Either of those would seem hopelessly out of place, so I go with the most direct route I can think of.

I take off my clothes.

Fishing out the five hundred-dollar bills you told me to bring, I fan them out on the dresser near the door. The smell of the money makes me even harder. My cock feels pained, desperate for your touch. Looking at the five bills, I walk back to the rumpled mess of my suit pants and fish out my wallet. I take out as many twenties as I can find, put ten of them crosswise atop the fanned hundreds. Consider it a tip—in good faith, because I know this is going to be the fuck of my life.

I decide to take a shower; I rinse off quickly, not bothering with soap, then towel dry as I drip my way to the bed. I toss the towel in the corner and peel back the covers. The sheets feel cold against my naked body, rough and starched against my cock. Every inch of my flesh feels alive with sensation and anticipation. My heart pounds as I await the arrival of my well-paid whore.

When I hear the key in the door, I can't help but squirm against the sheets. I think in that moment I want you more than I've ever wanted any woman in my life. My cock pulses with the sound of your key scraping in the lock.

You enter the dimly lit hotel room. When you pick up the money, you sigh.

"You're very generous, Mike," you tell me, tucking the bills into your purse. "Generous as well as handsome."

"Thank you."

"What do you want to do, Mike?"

"Make love to you."

You laugh, bringing your hand to your mouth as if you can't believe I've just said it. "Oh, Mike. I seriously doubt that."

"All right," I say. "I want to fuck you."

"Really. Is that all?"

"I want to fuck you so hard you scream," I say. "I want to fuck your pussy until you come so many times you cry."

You smile. "Does your girlfriend let you talk like that?"

"She encourages it."

"She must be a very naughty girl. Naughty and very, very horny."

"Exceptionally so, Simone."

You walk to the side of the bed, setting your purse on the dresser and shrugging off your little jacket. The dress clings to your breasts and I can see your nipples, erect with excitement. You come over to the side of the bed and bend down slightly, turning away from me.

"Unzip me, will you?" you ask, your voice soft and seductive.

I draw your zipper down to the small of your back, exposing the strap of your lacy bra. You walk around to the foot of the bed and peel the dress away, slowly revealing your body. God, it's incredible. I always want you when I see you take your clothes off, but now it's particularly acute—I'm practically insane with desire. Your black bra is cut so low and tight that your breasts are spilling out, your nipples having already made their way through the flimsy spray of lace on the edges of the half-cups. Your matching thong is skimpy and descends to the point where I could see your pubic hair if you hadn't trimmed so assiduously. The black garter belt frames your crotch deliciously, and I notice that you've put the thong on over your garters.

You crawl onto the bed, straddling me as you make your way up to me and pull down the sheets. Bending down, you brush your breasts against my chest, kissing my neck.

"I want you to fuck me," you whisper. "Any way you want. I'm yours for the night."

I wrap my arms around you and pull you tight to me. Our lips meet and I taste the vodka, lime and triple sec on your tongue. My hands cradle your bare ass and you push it back into my grasp, arching your back as you draw your breasts up to my face. I suckle your hard nipples gently as you reach under the sheets and take hold of my cock, wrapping your slender fingers around my shaft and squeezing. Hungrily, you begin to stroke me. Before I know it, you've buried yourself under the tangled sheets and I feel your mouth on my cock, hot and slippery. You take me into your mouth and your lips descend until they're almost wrapped around the base of my shaft. I reach out to grab your waist and guide you around. I pull down your thong and you wriggle out of it; I see that you're not only trimmed, you're shaved. You reverse your position on top of me and spread your legs around my face, gently settling your pussy onto my mouth. I taste your sharp, musky cunt and my tongue finds your clit, teasing it as I hear your moan muffled around the shaft of my cock. Your hips grind back and forth as my lips mold to yours, your juices flowing as your smooth pussy rides my face.

You take your time, because you're an expert. Certainly you know the exact way to make me come, but in this persona you know the way to make *any* man come, and it's clear you don't want me to come yet. Your mouth moves in just the right rhythm to get me close, bringing me to the edge of orgasm as your head bobs up and down on me. Then, without warning, you slow, or slip my cock out of your mouth and tease the head with the very tip of your tongue, letting me cool down so you can savor my hard cock for as long as you want. I, however, am not nearly so charitable. I want you to come, and come now, because I'm hungry to feel your body bucking on top of me, your hips pumping your cunt against my face as you desperately suck my cock. I focus on your clit, only licking down to your tight opening so I can taste the flowing juices of your pussy. You're wet, incredibly wet—I noticed that from the first moment your pussy touched my lips. And I can tell from the way you're moving that you're close; you're going to come.

Of course, I know it doesn't matter—a good whore will always fake an orgasm when her client is eating her out, won't she? Never having had such an experience, I savor the knowledge that even if you weren't going to come, you'd pretend—after all, I've paid for you to enjoy yourself even more than I've paid for me to enjoy myself, because my ego demands it; my ego demands that you come, moaning, on my face.

Except that I know you could never fake it as good as you'd have to fake it to convince me, for real. I know you could never fake the way your whole body twists and writhes on top of me, the way your mouth, anxiously seeking my cock, dissolves into a pair of lips thoughtlessly, hopelessly working without the barest hint of control. You could never fake the way your thighs tighten around my face, the way your back arches, the way your breath comes tight in your throat and you shiver on top of me.

You could never fool me with the way you come.

Or could you?

I don't care. For now, it's real, and I want it. I want it so bad I suckle your clit steadily through the whole mounting rise of your climax, my tongue seething against it as you whimper "I'm going to come...I'm going to come...don't stop!" and then your body goes taut, jerking wildly, and you push your cunt down onto my face so hard it hurts me, so hard it almost suffocates me as you pump your hips madly. When you slump forward onto me, my cock, slippery with your spit, presses between your breasts, rubbing on the satin lace of your bra. You're panting desperately. You sound like you're about to cry.

"Oh god...oh god," you moan. "Mike, you're so good...oh god, you eat pussy so good...where'd you learn to eat pussy like that?"

I place my hands on your hips, lift your body slightly so I can slide out from under you. My cock, hard and slick, glistening in the light from the nightstand, is ready for you.

"From my girlfriend," I say as I position myself behind you. "She's very demanding."

I don't tease you at all; I enter you in one thrust, because I can't stand to be outside of you for one more instant. Your pussy is so wet I can feel the juice dribbling out of it, so tight from your muscles clenching in orgasm that I almost have to force my cock in. But you gasp as I enter you, and you lift your ass in the air, pushing back onto me, shoving your tight pussy over my cock until I can feel the head grinding against your familiar cervix, until I can feel your lips stretched tightly around the base of my shaft. God, it feels incredible. Your pussy is so hot around my cock I feel I'm about to be burned, but that doesn't stop me from drawing back almost all the way and then fucking you, hard, a single thrust that sends a spasm through your gorgeous body and lifts your ass high as you leave your face pressed against the bed and reach back with your hands to spread your lips wide for me, inviting me deeper.

I thrust into you again, hard, and your legs spread farther, your feet kicking involuntarily and sending the pillows flying to opposite sides of the room. The next thrust brings your ass up still higher, elicits a shuddering moan from your lips and I see a faint stain of spittle on the sheets as your tongue lolls out uncontrollably. You're still spreading your lips wide, begging me to enter you deeper, to fuck you harder. You whisper, "Yes...yes... yes...yes...god, Mike, your cock's so big, it's so fucking big I almost can't take it, Mike...god, it feels so good, so huge...your girlfriend's such a lucky girl, Mike, to have a guy with such a big cock...oh god, it's so huge...so fucking huge in my tight, wet pussy...."

Normally you would never moan like that in the middle of lovemaking; a woman entirely engrossed in the sexual sensations of the body, you limit your dirty talk to inarticulate moans and whimpers of pleasure, telling me all I need to know. But you've adopted the methods of your new persona, and while "Simone" is lifting her ass high to encourage me deeper into her pussy, she's also telling me how well hung I am. Strangely, the sound of your voice uttering such obscenities excites me more, and I start fucking you harder, faster, encouraged to new heights of need by each word you utter. I know I'm going to come soon, but I want my whore to come, too, to come on my cock as I thrust into her, feeling her pussy clench tight around my shaft. I reach under you and find your clit with my fingertips, its familiar contour inviting a familiar stroke. But Simone is a different woman, and you whisper "Oh god...rub me harder, harder, Mike, rub my clit harder, fuck me harder, fuck my wet pussy harder with your big fat cock!" I don't think I've ever heard you say the words *wet pussy* or *big fat cock* in all the time we've been together, and the filthiness, the silliness of it, draws me further into the illusion. I start rubbing your clit so hard I'm afraid I might hurt you, fucking you so hard I *know* I'm going to hurt you if I keep going—but you just beg me for more, encouraging me deeper into my passion as you pump back against me, your hands long since having left your pussy lips, no longer holding them open, knowing I need no encouragement to slide my cock deep into you. Now, your hands are flat against the bed, helping to push you back onto my cock, to meet every thrust I give you with one of your own, equally hard, equally demanding. Coaxed by the pressure on your clit and the familiar curve of my cock against your G-spot, you're going to come and I know it. And this time, as before, I'm quite sure you're not faking.

You tell me every sensation as it goes through your body. "I'm coming, Mike...fuck...I'm coming on your huge cock, coming—you're hitting my G-spot, Mike, you're hitting me deep—fuck me harder, fuck me harder!" And then your potty mouth disintegrates into incoherent moans of ecstasy, as I feel the muscles of your pussy contracting in rapid motions around my cock, milking me, begging me for my come even as you climax yourself, moaning on my cock.

I can't hold back any longer. My fingers still working your clit in time with the thrusts of our sweat-slick bodies, I match the rhythm of my hips to my own needs, the exact speed that will make me come—and within a few more thrusts, I'm doing it, coming deep inside you, hearing you beg for it—"Come inside me, Mike, come inside me, oh yes, give me your come!"—as I let go. When I go rigid and then relax on top of you, I feel my body sliding effortlessly against yours, both of us sheened with sweat. I kiss the back of your neck.

"Your girlfriend's very lucky," you sigh. "What's her name?"

"Simone," I tell you.

You laugh.

"What a strange coincidence. The same name as me."

"Isn't it, though?"

I get a wake-up call at 7:00 the next morning—the exact time I would normally get up for work.

You're gone, a faint depression in the bed where your naked body stretched out next to mine exhausted after we'd made love for the third time—a mere three hours ago. There's a note, written on hotel stationery in handwriting I don't recognize. Neat trick, that.

> *If you ever need company when you're in town, give*
> *me a call, Mike. I had a great time. Your girlfriend's a*
> *very lucky lady. Hope it lasts.*
> *Love,*
> *Simone*
> *XXXOOOXXX*

Underneath is written a phone number with a pager code. It's none of the numbers you use, not your work pager, home phone or cell phone.

Under the note is your skimpy black lace thong, still moist with the juice of your pussy

I resist the urge to call you all day, but I'm a little surprised that you don't call me. When I get back to my apartment from work that evening, though, I recognize a telltale scent in the air—your scent, not Simone's. The scent I recognize as your signature, the one I savor as it lingers in my apartment for hours after you've left.

The door to my bedroom is closed.

There on the coffee table are five hundreds, fanned out. Across them is a stack of twenties, and when I count them, I find there's $400, an extra ten $20 bills from what I tipped you.

I smile to myself and look at the closed bedroom door. Tucking the bills into my pocket, I unknot my tie.

Clearly you've changed the rules of the game, and upped the ante.

But then, the stakes were always higher than a simple seven hundred dollars.

I strip off my clothes and walk, nude, into the bedroom.

CALL ME 8

Connect with Phone Sex

*Humans are the only animal who can have sex
over the phone.*

—**David Letterman**

The phone is one of my personal favorite sex toys. No, I don't
like to fuck it, but I do have more than my fair share of
fun with my cell. Why do I like the phone so much? Well, first
there's phone sex. You know, your regular, everyday, call her up
at work, get him during the commute, let your fingers do the
walking while you're out grocery shopping with other customers
all around you phone sex, like in this sizzling story, "Wake-Up
Call," by Aimee Nichols:

"Hello?" The voice sounded huskier than usual.

"I'm ringing from work."

"Hi, honey," Lana answered lazily. "You woke me up. I was

just in the middle of a wonderful dream where I was Angelina Jolie's erotic maidservant. I seem to recall a lot of knives."

"Sorry," Emma murmured. *"I thought you'd be up by now."*

"It's all right, baby. What can I do for you?" Emma felt a jolt go straight to her clit, and her nipples hardened under her white cotton bra and regulation crisp white shirt. She crossed her free arm over her chest, certain people would notice. This was totally wrong. If anyone even suspected what she was about to do, she'd be fired on the spot.

And then there's don't-answer-the-phone sex, where you let the phone ring and ring, and she presses her pussy against that vibrating phone and turns the device into a toy, like in "Unlimited Minutes" by Elspeth Potter:

Ella called Julie on her cell phone.

"I'm on the train," Julie said. "I've been carrying the phone in my front pocket, like you told me to."

"Put it back now," Ella commanded. "Don't answer it."

Julie blew gently into the receiver. "I'm going to need a new battery again," she said, and hung up.

Ella pressed redial. The phone rang for a long time. Could Julie's seatmate hear the phone's rumble? Was her pocket vibrating? Would the plastic smell of arousal?

Then Julie answered. "I almost screamed that time," she murmured. "Call me again before I get to Boston."

There's long-distance phone sex, where you're aware you're paying twelve dollars a minute to get off, but you don't give a fuck.

And phone sex with an unsuspecting cold caller, like in Xavier Acton's hysterical and sexy "This Call May Be Monitored":

"Telemarketing is very naughty."

Rick paused. "Um...well, Ms. Dominica, I would be happy

to tell you about some of our excellent term life insurance products—"

"Telemarketing is very, very, very naughty, Rick. And I told you to call me Mistress."

Rick went to say something but his throat closed up. He finally managed to squeak: "Mistress."

"Very, very naughty. Do you like being naughty, Rick?"

Ms. Dominica's voice was thick, rich, powerful. When she chuckled, it sounded menacing.

"Ms. Dominca, if you'd allow me to take just a moment of your time, I could tell you about some of our excellent term life insurance products—"

"Do you know what I do to little boys who are naughty, Rick? Little boys who telemarket?"

"Ummmmm..."

"Let me tell you what I use this line for, Rick. This is an unlisted number because I advertise it only in certain publications for naughty men. Those men call me and beg me to punish them. And none of them has done anything nearly as naughty as telemarketing."

Rick cleared his throat. "Ms. Dominica—"

"Mistress Dominica!" she snapped.

The offshoots of phone sex are equally delicious. Blackberry sex, Skype sex, video-conferencing sex, old-fashioned pay phone or phone booth sex (if you can find one), and text sex, like in Rita Winchester's "Night Shift":

I groped in the dark and found my cell phone. I flipped it open, started texting.

CAN'T SLEEP. YOU THERE?

It didn't take long. A minute or two and my phone belched out a little jingle that told me I had a text message.

RIGHT HERE. ALL ALONE. NEED SOME HELP?

I smiled. The smile held the fear and worry at bay just a little, enough that I felt some of the tension uncoil, felt a fluttering in my belly at nothing more than little blue words on a white screen.

ALWAYS. CAN I COME?

I hit SEND *and closed my eyes. I let the anxiety sweep over me and then recede on its own. Like a tide, it moved over me, crushing me; receding, releasing me. It was awful but fixable.*

The lilting jingle told me to check my phone.

I KNOW YOU CAN COME. YOU'VE PROVEN IT. GET UP HERE. I'M LONELY.

But what else can you do with a phone?

In my never-have-the-same-sex style, I think the possibilities are almost as endless as the types of cell phone plans available. First, you can play with locations. Make a date to talk on the phone and think all morning about what's going to happen when that phone rings. Anticipation is one of the hottest turn-ons available—and it's totally free. If you know someone is going to call you up and get you off, chances are you'll be 90 percent of the way to the finish line before the phone rings.

Where to do this? The more unusual location the better, in my kinky opinion. At the Laundromat. In line at the movies. While delivering coffees to your office mates. In the elevator on the ride up. In the subway on the evening commute.

But you don't have to be by yourself to have phone sex. A phone is one of those toys you can play with together, and you don't even need to break out the bottle of lube. Try this: Each of you have a cell in hand. Then tell what dirty things you are going to do to one another, and don't hang up until you cannot stand to wait another second.

Ready for the bonus round?

Play the same game, but do it in public. At opposite sides of a café or restaurant, talk dirty to one another on the phone, pretending you are complete strangers. See which one of you caves first and heads to the restroom—and if it's a single stall with a lock, you can move right on to having sex in public.

But here's my favorite phone sex game: trying to stay calm while being fucked, and doing so while talking on the phone. Talking to whom? Your best friend. Your boss. Your florist. Your dentist; I don't care. This my favorite phone sex fantasy. I guess this isn't actually phone sex. It's *getting fucked while on the phone* sex.

And trust me, it's divine.

1-900-FANTASY

Dante Davidson

an and I found each other at a bar in Hollywood called Ye Olde Rustic Inn. It wasn't like a 1940s movie where our eyes met and held and we fell in love. It was more a floundering lunge together out of sheer necessity. Most of the other patrons were die-hard drinkers, decades older than the two of us (some older than the two of us put together).

Ian and I gravitated to each other as if pulled by a magnetic force. In the dimly lit bar, we moved from the counter to a booth in the back, and we got to know each other over a few unhurried shots of hard liquor.

He was trying to obliterate a pretty waitress named April from his memory. I was trying to erase the fact that a handsome truck driver named Miles even existed. Together, we sat in the deep, dark vinyl booths and drank Wild Turkey and talked about the very love affairs we were doing our best to forget. We covered reasons for the breakups, and we discussed what it was about our mutual exes that we missed the most.

On that first night together, I took one of his hands in mine and turned it faceup.

"Are you a palm reader?" he asked.

"An amateur."

"What do you see in my future?"

"It's cloudy," I said, "but I can see your past. Lonely nights. Lots of them. Trying to forget—"

"Her smile," Ian would say some evenings. "Her smell," he'd say on others. "The way she looked at me when we weren't talking, you know, just sitting at some café. She'd look at me like she loved me."

"She did."

"And then I ruined it."

By having a fling with her sister, so there truly was no going back.

When it was my turn to share, I'd feel slightly less poetic than Ian. Mainly, I missed Miles's cock. And although I had been the one to officially end the relationship, it had been his mean streak that had instigated the breakup.

At some point, Ian and I realized we were talking less about our exes and more about each other. We realized we were sitting closer together in the booth, that our legs just happened to bump and our thighs would rub as if our bodies had wills of their own. Weeks after our first meeting, I took his hand in mine again.

"What do you see this time?" he asked. "Still only my past?"

I shook my head. "There's a tigerish redhead in your future," I told him, and that led him to finally ask me back to his apartment at closing time. We walked the few blocks in silence, a strange occurrence for us. We were drinking buddies and talking buddies. Silence was new, startling, and difficult to deal with.

At his place, he ushered me in ahead of him and turned on the light. It was a small apartment, immaculate, with very few personal objects. Once we were inside, he took me to the sofa and then got a bottle and two glasses. Just because we'd left the bar didn't mean we were done drinking for the night. I was happy to have a glass in my hand again. It made me feel secure.

Ian settled himself on the other end of the couch and looked at me. I could suddenly relate to the way he'd said April had looked at him. He was staring, as if mesmerized, and I had to ask, "What?"—smoothing my hair, wondering if I looked worse to him out of the dim light of the bar.

"You're beautiful," he said, as if awed. "You're spectacular." I relaxed and regarded him. Ian has blond curly hair and green eyes, a strong jaw, a lopsided grin. He nudged me with his foot and I settled back into the sofa, still staring at him. We'd never had a difficult time with words, not until now, and I wondered how we were going to get over our new shyness.

Ian seemed to be wondering the same thing, or focusing on the same problem, because he stood and got his cordless phone, then came back to the sofa.

"I've gotten sort of addicted to nine-seven-six numbers since the breakup," he said, something he hadn't told me before. "I've been thinking of blocking them from my phone, it's that bad."

I tilted my head at him, curious. "I've never called one before."

"They're sort of fun," he said, placing the phone at his side, reaching for my hand. I felt a charge when he began playing with my fingertips, tickling them with his. "I don't talk to the same girl, or anything. But I always get off, listening."

I felt myself growing aroused, unsure of the exact reason for the wetness in my panties. I thought for a moment, then said, "I'd like to listen while you talk on one. That is, if you wouldn't mind?"

His eyes glowed. I think he'd had the same idea. I asked

next, "Do you have a separate line I could listen in on?" His studio was so small that I doubted he'd need two phones, but he surprised me by handing me the one at his side and returning with a second.

"I have one in the bedroom and one in the kitchen." He was dialing while he spoke. I lifted my receiver but he said, "I'll tell you when." Then, after a few moments, he nodded and I pressed the red button on my handset.

The woman's voice was low and husky, exactly how I would talk if I were working a sex line. I knew her goal was to keep Ian on as long as possible, and she did a good job, starting slow, asking him his name, describing herself for him, then asking his fantasy.

"Two women," he said, immediately.

"Oh," she purred. "Me and a friend of mine? Or do you have someone in mind?"

"I have someone," he said, and he moved closer to me on the sofa. He was gripping the phone with one hand, but he stroked his fingers up and down my thighs with the other.

"What's her name?"

"Miranda."

"Pretty name. Is she a pretty girl?"

"Spectacular," he said, his mouth was away from the phone, his lips against my ear as he spoke.

"What do you see us doing?" she asked.

"Why don't you tell me," Ian suggested, now being more forward, cradling the phone against his shoulder and sliding both hands under my skirt. I trembled as his fingertips met my naked thighs, swallowed hard as he dragged his thumb down the sopping wet seam of my panties.

"I see us in a tub," she said, "a bubble bath. Do you like that?"

"Mmm-hmmm," Ian murmured, to keep her going.

"The three of us soaping each other all over." She was getting a little louder as she spoke, as if she were really turning herself on.

"I like that," Ian said, then looked at me and mouthed the words, "Do you like it?" and I nodded.

His fingers were probing farther, up to the top of my panties, and he was sliding those down my thighs and off. The woman was still talking but I could hardly concentrate on what she was saying. Ian went on his knees on the carpet, between my thighs, and he set the phone down while he moved forward to taste me. I spread my legs wide and tried to stifle the moans I so wanted to let loose.

She was still describing the scene for us. "Your girlfriend is sitting on the edge of the tub, Ian. Her pussy needs to be shaved. Do you wanna shave it or should I?"

I tapped Ian's shoulder, wanting him to pick up the phone and talk, but he shook his head, the movement spiraling me into bliss as his whiskers tickled my outer lips. "You do it," he murmured against my skin. "You talk."

"This is Miranda," I said into the phone, startling the sex lady from her monologue. "Could you shave me? Ian's a bit busy...." The girl was good. She didn't falter. "Of course, darling. What color fur do you have down there?"

"Red," I said, sighing as Ian stroked it with his fingers, tugged gently on my curls. "Dark red."

"Pretty," she said, "But I'm gonna shave it all away and make you nice and clean for your man and me. I'm dying to taste you, and I want you bare before I give you my tongue. Would you like to be all nice and clean and pretty for me?"

I mumbled something, and she kept talking. Now I was having a hard time concentrating; between Ian and his magic tongue between my legs and this phone sex lady and her hypnotic voice, I felt transported. As I neared orgasm, I handed the phone to Ian, insisting he take it from me, and he said, "Ginger? It's been a pleasure. We'll call you again."

And as he hung up the phone, I said, "Next time you'll listen while I work you." He smiled and let me know that would please him just fine.

I think we're both going to mend our broken hearts without a problem. I foresee a long and powerful love filled with sexual heat and fire in our future. I may be an amateur soothsayer, but I've got a real good feeling on this one.

9 | JUST SAY NO
Don't Have Sex

Celibacy is the worst form of self-abuse.
—Peter De Vries

You've confessed your dirty dreams, touched yourself, flirted madly, written lusty letters, time-traveled, phoned out, and set the stage for fireworks of pleasure. What's next on the agenda? Simple: don't have sex.

Yes, you heard me.

Ratchet up the stakes. Email madly. Phone. Text. But whatever you do, don't have sex. I hear you politely saying, "Excuse me? I thought this was a sex guide. What do you mean, *don't have sex?*"

Imagine the feeling in the base of your stomach when you see a lover after a long break, when the only thing you can think to do is rip off your partner's clothes. Here, let me explain with a snippet from my story, "You Can't Always Get What You Want," based in cold hard fact on the time my man was in the former Soviet Union for six months.

By the time Sam arrived back in the states, he'd lost fifteen pounds, a bit of his sanity, and every last ounce of willpower. He'd promised you from a pay phone during a stopover at the airport in New York City that he was going to do two things before you even left the airport: fuck your ass, and spank your bottom until it was raw and red and cherry-perfect. You couldn't have been more excited to have both of those things happen.

Finally, you were going to get what you wanted! He was going to quick-step you back to the truck and take care of you in the way you'd been dreaming of for months now. But when Sam walked up the ramp, everything changed. He didn't smile. He didn't kiss you. He grabbed your hand and dragged you outside, into the muggy Los Angeles air. He chose a spot behind a pillar, where a concrete planter was half-filled with dying flowers. He set down his huge camping-style backpack filled with all of his possessions from his trip, filled with everything he hadn't given away to people who needed things more than he did if you want to talk just a little bit about "need"—and he sat down on the edge of the planter, hauled you over his lap and lifted your silly little Catholic schoolgirl skirt that you'd thought he'd find so sexy. While taxis vied for curb space, he pulled your white panties down your thighs and began to punish your ass for you right there, on the cigarette butt–littered sidewalk of LAX. And you thought for about half a second that you were in public with your bare-naked ass showing, and you thought for another half a second that someone was going to call the police or that people were going to complain.

And then Sam wrapped his hand in your hair and pushed your head down and continued to spank your ass in rapid, smarting strokes until you forgot to think about anything except the pain flaring through you and the fact that you'd been longing for a real spanking; not a pat-a-cake spanking, but a real, serious spanking for what felt like forever.

Still, you had some sense of decorum left in you, and you said, "Sam, the truck's just over—"

"Bad girls get punished in public all the time," Sam hissed, interrupting you. "Nobody says anything about it. Why should anyone say anything about you? Besides, people see worse every day in Los Angeles."

And you supposed he was right, because nobody did anything.

This is the type of immune feeling two people have when they haven't fucked for too fucking long.

Luckily, you can get that feeling without leaving the country. Just taunt each other fiercely. Play the flirt. Tease mercilessly. But, whatever you do, do *not* give in.

Of course, sometimes couples don't have much of a choice about not getting it on, like in my story "When Everyone Was Fast Asleep." Abstinence makes the heart grow fonder, or the cock grow harder, the pussy wetter. Something like that:

Staying with relatives can be extremely trying, especially when those relatives are your in-laws. Especially when those in-laws place you and your husband in separate bedrooms. Colin and I couldn't understand it. Here we were, newlyweds, forced to sleep divided by a long, dark hallway and a set of creaky stairs.

"Why?" I asked him. "We're married."

"But they know we don't plan on having kids right away," Colin said. "My mother thinks it's indecent. If we had a room with twin beds, like theirs, she might allow it."

"This is nuts," I said.

"That's why I didn't introduce you to them until we were

engaged." He laughed when he said it, but I could tell that he was only halfway kidding.

After a week of celibacy, we made a pact to meet at midnight in the backyard. I climbed out of my bedroom window, feeling akin to Juliet, and met my waiting Romeo down below. Knowing the alleyways of his youth, Colin led me to a nearby park. Neither of us spoke on the walk, but he held my hand and brought it to his lips, kissing each one of my fingertips.

The park was deserted at the midnight hour, and we quickly joined on one of the swings, rocking together in a perverted seesaw fashion to a fast and furious orgasm. Then, with the moonlight on our skin, with the prospect of another week of celibacy stretching out before us like a prison sentence, we began to play.

Whether circumstances keep you apart, or you decide to refuse temptation on your own—the results will be the same: a windfall of pleasure when skin finally meets skin. The last time Sam and I played this game, I think we were able to hold out for seven or eight days. (Or was it hours?)

For extra credit, if you really want to enhance the concept of not having sex, consider a chastity belt, like the one in my story "Breaking the Rules":

Now, I swallowed hard, and I could feel myself growing wet under the chastity belt. Jack ran his hand over his short dark hair, as if he were contemplating his next move. He had a wolfish expression on his face, and I tried to read the look in his eyes, but failed. All I could think about was how turned on I was...and would continue to be for four more days. There was no release in sight.

No relief at all.

When you are finally ready to fuck, you'll be so ready you'll be able to taste the pleasure in your mouth. And perhaps that's where you'll decide to start.

EROTIC FICTION

NOT TONIGHT

Mathilde Madden

K nocking on her door was always the most frightening part.

His heart hammered, just as it always did. He swallowed gently and stood up straight, just as he always did. But when she opened the door, everything was different.

"Not tonight," she said, without any sign of regret. And then the door closed again.

Taken aback, he stood for some time, staring at the woodgrain of her front door; not quite able to believe it. Steeling himself—finally—with something that was more desperate desire than real courage, he took hold of the door handle and turned. It wasn't locked.

Uninvited and uncommented upon he walked into her hallway. 'What did you say?" he called, sounding far sharper than he meant to, than he would have dared to.

There was no reply. So he went to find one.

He found her in the study; in half dark. The only illumination in the room came from a small lamp on the desk, which was making a pool of light on her paperwork and sparkling glints in her hair and the rims of her spectacles.

She didn't even look up. "I said 'Not tonight.' " He could hear her gritted teeth. "It's just not a good time."

He stepped into the room and pushed the study door closed behind him. This place looked so ordinary, even in semidarkness, and yet this was the room she also used as his torture chamber. There was the corner where she would make him stand and face the wall, his trousers lowered so she could see the marks her cane had left. And under that covered table he knew there was a cage, which was too small and caused cramps in his long limbs and muscular shoulders. It was too dark to see the iron rings that she had had sunk into the walls months ago; high enough that if she manacled his wrists to them he would be forced up onto tiptoes.

In this room of all places, it was impossible for him to let it go. "But it's Wednesday," he said.

She still didn't look up from her desk. "I know perfectly well what day of the week it is."

"Sorry." He creased his brow. He felt himself growing more petulant by the minute. It was all he could do not to stamp his foot. Stamp his foot or get down on his knees. "What's wrong?"

She sighed and finally looked up at him. The light caught her face then, and he caught his breath. "Nothing, I'm just tired. I don't have the energy tonight." She did look tired.

He cocked his head and fixed his coyest expression. He lived for Wednesday nights. Work had been hell these last few months and he didn't think he could bear to trudge back into London without some kind of tension release. "You don't have to do anything," he said, very gently, "I'll wait on you. Please."

"I said 'No.' "

He swallowed and moved closer to the desk until he was near enough to rest his palms on the top. "But why? You know you want to."

She held his gaze. "Don't tell me what I want. You are really pushing your luck now."

"Am I? What are you going to do about that?" He lifted one knee onto the desktop and lowered his gaze, deferent and needy and hard. Ready.

Her expression was unreadable. "Do you take me for some kind of fool? I told you. Now leave."

"Make me," he hissed, hoping that his banging heart wasn't audible as he raised his other knee, and gingerly climbed up to kneel on her desk.

She fixed his gaze with flashing eyes as their faces drew level. "No."

"You want to though don't you? Listen to how I'm talking to you." He gulped quickly. "Surely you can't let it go unpunished. You can't tell me you don't want to hear me scream right now."

"Is that a fact?" And then, just as he thought he might have to give up, came a tiny half smile, just a flash that was thought better of, but a flash nonetheless. She was teasing back, even if she didn't mean to, and he rose to the challenge.

"Oh you know it is. You really ought to beat me. You ought to beat me harder than you did last week. What you did to me last week was..." He paused while he searched for the perfect word. "Last week was amazing. Although I don't know how I bore it. I was almost at my limit. The marks lasted for three days, you know. I could barely sit down. It's a good job my boss wasn't around to wonder why I was using the mantelpiece as a desk."

He allowed himself a little internal smile as he saw her pupils dilate a little.

"Really?" her voice had a little shake to it now. "You couldn't sit at your desk?"

He knelt up on the desk and took hold of his collar, opening the top button, suggestively. "No, I couldn't, I was far too sore." He popped open another button. Then another.

"Well it's a good job you like frustration," she said, taking his hands and stopping him before he undid the fourth button, "because I have no intention of hurting you, tonight..."

Barely before she finished speaking he pushed her hands away from his shirt, leaning across the desk and placing a pale finger across her lips. "Because you'd rather be using me?" He punctuated the question with a flash of raised eyebrow and a slow smile. "Perhaps you'd prefer me on my knees tonight. Taking off your knickers with my teeth—because you know that my tongue works so much better if my wrists are bound behind my back. If I'm helpless as you tear at my hair and force me against you, raping my face until you are satisfied. Jerking your hips against me so I know for certain that you own me. That I know for certain I'm yours and I come all over the floor without even touching myself. Like the filthy bastard I am."

She reached out and took his hand gently, pushing it away from her lips. "Well it seems you have even more of a talented tongue than I ever realized. I can't imagine who taught you to talk like that, though. You must be getting out and about in the big city."

"Oh no, I never go out. I stay at home every night and think of you. No one else has shaped my desire."

"Really, well I must make a note to leave you ungagged next time we play so you can put that verbal talent to good use. But not tonight. You know you really do need to learn restraint."

"Teach me about restraint then. If I'm bothering you, you know how you can stop me. Tie me up out of your way, chain me to the bed, lock me in your broom cupboard, strip me and cage me and leave me until morning. Make me an object. Make me your property. Own me. Oh god, please."

A breathless pause, and when she spoke again her voice was very low. "You know, you don't need to do this to make me want you."

He blinked, but continued his pleading, his voice cracking now with desperation and desire. "You don't have to tie me then. I don't need ropes or chains or bars to obey, give me the order and I'll face the wall until morning. Please. I don't need to come, I don't even need to touch you, but please. I just need you to own me."

She stared at him, a distant look in her eyes.

"I'll do anything. Anything you want. No safeword."

She held up both her hands. "Stop, please. It's not you. You've done nothing wrong. Do you think I'm tired of you? I could never grow tired of you. I need to..." She trailed off. "Just not tonight."

He stared at her. He tried to do that intense look that she seemed to find so easy, and he said again, "Please. I'll do anything."

"Anything?"

"Anything."

"Then go home."

KISS, LICK, SUCK 10

Be an Oral Authority

I think pop music has done more for oral intercourse than anything else that ever happened—and vice-versa.

—Frank Zappa

I'd be willing to put money where my mouth is that most lovers appreciate oral sex. (I know several women who have told me that their all-time most memorable orgasms occurred when their partners went down on them.) What's more dreamy than licking, and then sucking, even slurping when the heat begins to build? Warm skin and a hot, wet mouth... Man, I'm getting a little hungry myself. I mean, just consider this scene from Thomas S. Roche's "Parts of Heaven":

I'm groaning and rocking up and down, pumping my hips back and forth while Angel rides me like a vixen. I start to whimper. I throw my head back and almost scream, the hottest orgasm of my life exploding through my cock and into Angel's mouth. I shudder and thrash back and forth, and Angel holds on for dear life, her lips clamped around the head of my cock as she milks me. Finally, my spasms subside and my head slumps forward.

In "All-Day Sucker" by Jacqueline Pinchot, two hungry women feast on one another:

They spread themselves out, luxuriously, on the table and dined upon each other's cunts; savoring the difference in their flavors, the lingering full-bodied aroma. Like connoisseurs of fine wines, they murmured descriptions to each other: "Warm and sweet..."

"Rich and delicious..."

"Like licking an all-day sucker."

That was Clarice's summation of Emma's cunt, and she couldn't get it out of her mind. Not even as her fingers joined in and probed Emma deeply. Not even as Emma, setting her own rhythm, locked her lips to Clarice's clit and sucked and tickled and lapped...

P. S. Haven's "Westbound" features a blow job outdoors, by the side of the road:

He surrendered. "I want you to." And she gulped his cock into her fever-hot mouth. Richie moaned pitifully as she sealed her wet lips around him and slid them down the entire length of his shaft with maddening patience. His cock tasted good, and it felt good in her mouth. He smelled like gasoline. Not the watered-down, 90-something octane you got nowadays, but the good stuff. The leaded stuff. 104-octane. The kind that burned clean and pure. Sky Chief. Hi-Test. Fill'er up.

She swallowed, trying to take him all the way into her mouth, trying to devour him. It was like it was happening to somebody else, like a slow-motion movie. His hands crawled around her

neck and held her there and his hips bucked up hard, and he
pulled her down and plunged the full length of his cock, all of
it, into her throat.

"Good Kitty" by Shanna Germain is sure to get anyone hard
or wet (or harder or wetter):

I suck on the shirttails that hang on either side of his cock,
letting my tongue feel the rough fabric. With the fabric on my
tongue, I lick him again, just to see if he likes the way it feels,
like a wet kitty tongue. He hisses between his teeth and his cock
jumps.

When I take all of him inside my mouth again, he puts his
hands around my throat. Not hard, but like a temporary collar.
Like a way to claim me for now.

Sometimes even the mere *thought* of being lapped at is enough,
as in Michael Hemmingson's hysterical yet sexy "Fans":

"I have three fans blowing on me," I say.

"You and your groupies," she says.

We're talking on the phone. It's an unbearably hot summer
in Southern California.

"I like that image," she continues, "three of them taking
turns blowing you. Or maybe the other two are each licking you
like kittens."

"Ah, now, that would be nice. But it would be nicer," I say,
"if you were—"

But as relationships progress, often oral activities are rele-
gated to foreplay. Why not give this tantalizing act top billing?
Spend a few nights learning (or relearning) how to please one
another with your lips, teeth, and tongue.

Start with licking, like in Rachel Kramer Bussel's appropriately named "Dangerous":

Lucy looked right at me, her eyes knowing, and took her
tongue and deftly licked one nipple and then the other. When

she looked back at me, her eyes had gone back to that studied
innocence, part pout, part come-on. "I won't tell if you won't
tell," she said in a voice that almost made me come right there.

From licking, move to sucking, as in "His Hands" by Sharon
Wachsler:

I feel like I've waited years for this moment. I suck greedily
at your hand in my mouth. Your other fist has the back of my
hair, guiding my head back and forth, as if I were giving you
a blow job. I can only groan around it and grind against you,
feeling you sliding in and out of me. I engulf you from both
ends. Your grunts and moans are lost in my screams. Pounding
in and out—your hands and your cock—the slippery friction,
the heat, my swollen clit: I lose track of time.

Did you catch the similarities in the previous snippets?
Neither one dealt with mouth-to-groin activities. Sometimes,
I think lovers forget that oral sex can include licking (or
sucking or slurping) any body part. There is no need to beeline
directly to your partner's cock or clit. Go slow. Lick the base
of the neck, the webbing between thumb and pointer, the
indent at the hip.

Then from sucking, well, it's just natural to progress to
slurping, like in this delicious scene by Erica K. from "What
Makes a Slut a Slut":

"You're quite a little cocksucker," she said. "But you know
what makes a slut a real slut?"

The first was a reasonable comment, since I had her cock
down my throat at the time. My answer was, therefore, slow
in coming. I eased myself back, opening up wide, letting
my ravaged throat give up the feel of the cock it so loved.
The slim, arrow-shaped head popped out of the back of
my throat and I gave a little shudder as I came up, gasping for
air. A string of saliva popped and glistened between my lips,

which were painted bright red with a thick coating of lipstick.
I slurped.

"No, Mistress," I told her, even though I already knew.

Remember, go slow. Enjoy every single moment. Work up to sixty-nining. And then work back down to one again.

FILTHY

Sommer Marsden

H is first licks are the slowest. He drags his tongue across my clit so slowly my breath hisses in and out of me. He places deliberate kisses along the inside of my thighs.

"I'm going to fuck you, Sara. But first I'm going to eat you. Will you go all soft and warm and wet for me?"

As soon as he says it, I do. My body loosens and goes fluid. It doesn't matter that once upon a time words like that would have made me blush. Or tell him to hush. They would have mortified and terrified me. Then I met Adam. Now the words, even what had once been considered the filthiest of words, resonate like the most beautiful music in my ears.

His tongue darts over the hardened nub of my clit until I think I might scream but I love it.

"I can see you clenching. Your cunt. It gets very greedy when I eat you. It contracts and relaxes like it's beckoning me. It flutters and pulses." He sticks his tongue into my cunt and I shudder. "Get messy for me, Sara. Will you? I like to wear you on my face from ear to ear. I like the smell of your pussy in my hair and on my skin. I like it seeping out of my pores when I'm done. I want to swallow you and wear you...and then I'll fuck you."

I can feel my body tightening. Between the words and his tongue my heart is doing a drunken staggering dance in my chest.

"I remember when just the word *pussy* would make you blush. Shake your head. So very proper, you were. Those words were not to be spoken aloud. Shouldn't even be thought. Do you remember the first time I told you that you had a beautiful cunt? I thought you would faint. But now you blossom when I throw filthy words out into the air. You like to gather them like butterflies. And when I give them to you, when I heap praise upon your cunt and your ass and whatever other filthy thing that comes to mind...ah, you simply open up like an exotic flower."

I try to say something but all that comes out is a low needy moan. A sound that speaks volumes: Please.

"Get messy for me, Sara. Yes, baby, give it to me," Adam whispers, "but not yet." Then he chuckles and darts his tongue to the crux of my thigh.

I hang there, on the edge of orgasm; waiting, panting, listening. I can hear the ceiling fan's low hum. I can hear a dog barking in the neighborhood. I can hear my heart pounding and the blood forcing its way through my veins. It's like the roar of a waterfall as I wait and silently demand more. More from him. More words.

Adam stares up at me from between my thighs, over my pubis. His green eyes flash with good humor and malicious intent. "Do you know what you taste like?"

I can only shake my head. My voice is gone.

"You taste like cinnamon and raspberries and what I imagine sunshine tastes like. That's what your cunt tastes like to me."

Then his tongue returns and before I can stop myself I arch up into him. Bang myself against his mouth. "Greedy girl," he murmurs as he laps at me.

The slide of his fingers entering my body is enough to tighten me further. It's nearly painful it feels so good. One finger, two fingers. "Should I go for a third?" The words vibrate over my clit, spiral down, warm me. I feel my body release another freshet of desire. And he hums with pleasure as he licks me clean. "See, when you do that I have to start all over. I need a clean canvas. I like to clean you up and then make you do it again. I like to watch you go from pristine to wet. From unmarred to saturated. How wet will you get for me, Sara? Get as wet as you want. I have all night to be down here, soaking you in. Licking you clean."

His fingers, long and blunt and talented, stroke me from the inside. He finger paints inside my body with slow deliberate strokes that make my body bow. He's playing me and painting me with his fingers. Little sparks of color ignite in the blackness behind my closed eyelids. I close my eyes. I keep my eyes closed so that when he speaks, it is that much louder, that much clearer.

"Third finger in. When you come for me, when I've had my fill, then I can fuck you. Slide my cock into this perfect wet heat of yours. Will you come for me, Sara? Will you? Will you come messy? Come sweet? Will you scream for me, Sara? Will you call my name?"

I'm nodding along with his words as if I'm keeping time with music. I will. All of those things. All of them and more. The sweetness is nearly unbearable. There are tentative flickers deep within me. An echo that happens to precede the sound. The distant beat of an orgasm that is about to come to fruition.

His fingers are swirling, pushing, probing. His tongue is a

moist wet violation. He suckles me in, rolling my clit over the tip of his tongue and I stop breathing. I just stop. And I listen because I am right there and one more divine string of words will do me in.

His tongue flickers and dances over my skin. "Come for me, Sara. Gush for me, Sara. Thrash for me, Sara. Sara who tastes like raspberries and cinnamon and sunshine."

And I do. Thrash for him, grab his hair and pull him close. Thrust up against his patient waiting mouth and beautiful lips. And he drinks me in and never stops talking. Words against flesh. Breath hot on my clit. Beautiful, filthy words spill from his lips as he drinks me in. And when he rises to get between my thighs, slides his cock into my waiting body and kisses me, he smells like me. Tastes like me. Me and filthy words.

11 | FOOD, GLORIOUS FOOD

Guess Who's Coming During Dinner?

Great food is like great sex—the more you have, the more you want.

—Gael Greene

Most of my guiltier pleasures revolve more around sugar than sex. This is because I tend not to feel guilty about what I do in bed, or up against the wall, or bent over the hood of a '65 Cadillac, while I do get a twinge of guilt at drowning my deadlines in dark red licorice.

Yet when I mix food with sex, the guilt disappears and the hot, melting chocolate pleasure remains. I'm a bit of a slut where food and sex are concerned. I like the concept of being eaten from—as if I've magically turned into a plate. And I like the concept of licking delicious sauces and creams off of my lover's body. I can even seriously understand the fun in the adorable "wet and messy" fetish called *sploshing.*

I'm not the only one who understands the appeal of having a little sex with your meal. Shanna Germain writes in "Kneading":

At home, I don't let her touch me. There is only this: my fingers tangled in her thin apron strings, cascade of cotton and flour against the floor, Macy's dark arms iced with sugars and spice. My recipe is simple: Macy and me, hands and skin, kneading and heat. The best recipes just taste complicated. This is something I plan to teach her.

And I've written about sex and Slurpees in "Cherry Slushee":

While I watched, he drew the Slushee in with the straw and used the flavored ice to decorate my skin—my nipples, my collarbones, a lone line down the basin of my belly.

"Oh, god—" I moaned.

He followed each magic line of the straw with the warmth of his mouth.

"Oh, yes—" I said next.

To my utter delight, he took turns, first drawing designs on my naked skin with the iced cherry confection and then retracing those same patterns with his tongue. I thrashed on the bedroll, made crazy by the combination of the cold and the heat, by the tempting slow way that he worked me. I couldn't decide what it was that I wanted—or more truly, I couldn't fathom that I really wanted what I thought I did. Which was this:

The Slushee, that cold, chilling Slushee, right on my clit. But, that's what I wanted. Even as I shivered all over, trembling with all my might, I desperately wanted him to lift the straw and streak a line of deep fuchsia iced Slushee over my clit.

"Do it," I told him. "Oh, please."

Andrea Dale describes a satisfying way to wake up in "Breakfast in Bed":

I must have been backlogged on needing sleep, because I didn't fall back into the dream, even though I'd hoped to. Nope, I slid right down into the full-on blackness of exhaustion.

I knew this because, when I slowly ascended through layers of consciousness, I discovered Cal had been very busy and I'd slept right through all of it.

Delicious aromas tickled my nose. Aw, he'd brought me break-fast in bed! Before I even opened my eyes, I started to sit up.

That's when I discovered that he'd also managed to tie my hands to the brass headboard.

Sometimes when good sex and good meals are combined, it's difficult to tell exactly what is being written about—food or fucking—like in the deliciously dirty "Cock Lobster" by Ann Rosenquist Fee:

It's got nothing to do with "cock," with prancing feathers and farm stink. Nor does it match "pork," or its progeny, "wiener," a too-smooth tube like latex stuffed with scraps of hog lips and assholes. Least of all is it like "beef," a flat slab or a patty that bleeds like a woman.

It's like something else. It's a thing caught and caged the whole long day, caught in the cool dark till dinnertime. Until somebody's hungry.

It's a thing that's best cooked alive. A thing to crack from its shell—from denim or khaki—and from its soft undershell as well—sometimes cotton—cracked open with skillful hands. With practiced fingers that move from shell to bucket without spilling a drop, deft, slippery, fast. Shell cast aside to bare flesh in ridges, in fibers, pale silk stretched over stone, a blue-green spine soft underneath.

It's a thing that tears if teeth go that far. If teeth can bear it. If teeth are allowed to do what they want, to sink deep into the silk and the sinew.

The temptation is to add butter from the plastic cup that comes with the order. But it's better without. It's got salt enough on its own, enough juice, the sweat that comes from fear of being torn apart.

When it's finished, the bodies around the table sigh. Smack their greasy lips. Check their faces for shreds of flesh. Roll away, slow, from the spreading puddle of melted butter and water from Casco Bay.

However you desire to dine (or be dined upon), you'll always want to save room for dessert, as demonstrated in "Choice of Toppings," by Jeremy Edwards:

The pleasant handwriting at the bottom of the ice cream parlor check was small, but perfectly legible:

Eat me?

It was a polite invitation, not a rude rebuff. And the question mark was as sinuously sexy as it was grammatically significant.

In the bottom right corner was a cute, curly little arrow in the same handwriting, meaning Over. *I hadn't noticed this before. Now I duly flipped the slip of paper.*

...with whipped cream?

it said on the back.

Why not write a sexy little invitation like this one? Be sure to stick the note where you know your lover will find it—maybe on the front of your shirt? Or the front of hers?

APPETIZERS

Simon Torrio

Standing before the wreckage, I feel an overwhelming wave of sadness that such a tragedy has come to pass. Sullied china scatters across a red-stained white cloth. Twisted metal implements are smeared with a curious mixture of colors. Candles stand like broken torches, guttered out at the height of their power by the sweep of human flesh in the throes of sudden helplessness. Fragrant flowers, ruined in their moment of triumph, lie sprawled across despoiled white, their translucent viscera running down, still, in diamond drops onto the floor.

Yet the tragedy persists: we didn't even make it to dessert.

Iris showed up at eight, eyes full with the emptiness of her belly. She'd worn a very tight dress as I requested: skintight and pale peach, plunging deep in the front and revealing the ripe orbs of her breasts. I wore a clean white apron, black slacks, a white shirt and black tie. I had a white cloth draped over one arm.

"Your table is ready, ma'am," I said to her. "May I take your coat?"

She smiled, amused at the costume I'd donned for the evening. She handed me her coat and I hung it in the closet near the front door. She followed me into the depths of my apartment, finding the table set with one place, the head of the table. I pulled out her chair and she sat down.

Before she'd had a chance to adjust herself, I seized her wrists and produced a pair of handcuffs from my apron pocket. She barely knew what was happening before I had her wrists cuffed to the back of the chair.

"Hey!" she said. "What's going on?"

"Dinner for one," I said. "Look, ma, no hands."

Her eyes narrowed and her face reddened slightly. I saw the peaks of her breasts begin to harden under the peach-colored dress. She relaxed, immobilized, into her chair.

"All right," she said. "I'll play. I'm hungry enough."

"Yes," I said, my open palm running down the front of her body and teasing her nipples to full erection. "I've been noticing that for weeks."

She moaned softly as I stroked her nipples gently. She squirmed slightly in her chair, and when I'd tormented her sufficiently for now I released her, coming around the side of the table and slowly screwing the corkscrew into the wine. I saw her eyes following the metal implement's entry into the resistant flesh of the cork with more than casual interest.

The sharp pop of the wine cork made her jump a little even though she was expecting it. I splashed wine into the glass and held it for her to sniff.

She did, and accepted the taste when I placed the smooth glass to her lips and tipped it.

"Excellent," she said.

"Very good, ma'am," I told her, and poured a full glass of wine. Her eyes lingered over it and I allowed her another tiny sip, going slow so as not to soil that perfect dress, before disappearing into the kitchen.

Her lips, glossed red with wine, parted slightly as her eyes devoured the bowl of soup I set before her.

"Carrot-ginger curry," I said. "Soup of the day. Did you know that ginger is reputed to be an aphrodisiac?"

"You don't say," she muttered, squirming slightly as she tested the strength of the handcuffs, the chair, her wrists.

"Yes. Furthermore, one Dr. Kellogg, who not incidentally invented the cornflake, thought spicy food like curry encouraged impure thoughts."

"Did he?" she murmured, looking perturbed.

"Yes," I said. "Let's find out if he was right."

I stood behind her, towering over her small form as I curved my arms around her and took up her soup spoon. I lifted a spoonful of bright orange soup to her lips, which she parted obediently for me. I blew on the soup to cool it, then slipped the tip of the spoon between her wine-reddened lips. She slurped appreciatively.

"Too hot?" I asked her.

"Spicy," she said. "But not hot."

"Story of my life," I told Iris, and gave her another liquid spoonful. I fed her the soup with my arms coiled around her, feeling the warmth of her body as the spicy soup raised her skin temperature and made sweat break out on her flesh. Still, she ate all her soup like a good little diner. I punctuated every few spoonfuls with a sip of red wine. With each shift of my arms, I could feel her wriggling in my grasp.

"Was the soup to your liking, ma'am?"

"Delicious," she said breathlessly, her mouth obviously hot from the curry.

I poured water from the clear pitcher and lifted the glass to her lips. She dribbled a bit and I licked the droplets from her chin. She moaned softly and parted her lips for a kiss that never came.

I slipped away and glanced back to see her bare shoulders shivering as I went into the kitchen.

When I returned I held a tiny dish, no bigger than a shot glass, filled with a brightly colored sorbet, arrayed on a small tray with a minuscule spoon.

"Passion fruit," I said. "A palate cleanser."

"Passion fruit?"

"Passion fruit."

I once again leaned over her, feeding her tiny nibbles of the sorbet from the very tip of the spoon. She sucked the confection into her mouth and swallowed greedily.

"Time for the next course," I told her without letting her finish the sorbet. She pouted noticeably and I leaned close to kiss those sorbet-shimmering lips, then pulled away at the last moment.

When I returned, I brought her appetizer: oysters in fennel-cream sauce.

"Don't tell me," she whispered as I leaned close. "Fennel's an..."

"Aphrodisiac," I said with a cruel smile. "Reputedly, at least. You learn quickly, ma'am. Open up."

I fed her each succulent oyster on the end of my best silver fork, teasing her lips gently and making her lean forward to get it. I could feel her heat rising, especially when her nipping teeth dislodged an oyster from the silver fork and made it fall to the chair between her slightly parted thighs.

"Ooops," I said, and dropped my hand between then, seizing the oyster. My hands lingered on the insides of her thighs, and I could feel her breath arrested as she waited for me to touch her.

I did not, and tucked the sullied oyster into my apron pocket.

I could see her pouting as I took away the empty plate. She'd finished all her oysters, like a good girl.

I returned with another sorbet—mango.

"I've always thought mango tastes suspiciously like..."

"Don't say it," she whispered, her lips parting.

This time I let her have the whole tiny scoop of sorbet, and she moaned softly as its sweetness cooled her mouth. Her lips were glossed bright orange and the sips of wine, she sucked at greedily—so greedily that droplets ran down her chin and onto her clothing.

"You've soiled this dress," I said.

"Oh," she whispered. "I guess I should run cold water through it."

"Yes," I told her. "I guess you should."

I unfastened her handcuffs and led her to the bathroom. I prepared the next course while I listened to the water running. When she emerged, I saw her face and cleavage were flushed, the latter made even more evident by the fact that she'd stripped off the dress and was now wearing only a white lace demi-bra and panties, white garter belt and white stockings.

I drew her hand to my face and licked her fingers. Under the clean tang of soap I could taste her. I pushed her against the wall, feeling her melt into my grasp.

"Did you make yourself come?" I asked.

She shook her head. "Uh-uh," she mumbled, almost sadly.

"Good," I told her.

I handcuffed her to the chair again and this time her squirming was even more adorable. She'd worn a very skimpy thong, and I knew the wooden chair must be cold on her buttocks. Her nipples, hard and pink, had begun to poke out over the lace tops of her bra cups.

I brought out the main course: sauteed salmon and eggplant with coconut sauce.

"Eggplant I know about," she said softly. "But is coconut an aphrodisiac?"

"No," I said. "They just look like a pair of really big balls."

I fed her each morsel without care to neatness; coconut sauce ran down her chin and onto the swell of her cleavage. I felt her squirming against me as I leaned heavily against her shoulders. After the third bite I abandoned the fork and plucked pieces of salmon and eggplant with my fingers, making her lean forward to get them and teasing her lips open with my fingers before letting my fingertips remain behind, stroking her tongue as she swallowed. Soon my hand and her face were both covered, shimmering and savory. I pressed my lips to hers and she once again melted into me, this time irrevocably, as my cock had begun to press so firmly against my apron that I knew I could stand no more.

"Fuck me," she begged. "Please don't make me wait."

My plans were decimated—I couldn't wait for dessert. I seized the key from my apron and undid one wrist of her handcuffs; she leapt from the chair and pushed herself against me before I could undo the other cuff, leaving the cuffs dangling half-open from her wrist. Her arms around me pulled me tight, and when I shoved her onto the table, neither of us hesitated or started at the sound of shattering china as we swept it to the floor.

I knocked the candles out of the way just in time to avoid setting her hair on fire. Glancing behind her, I was relieved to see they'd gone out as they tumbled. I was glad, now, that I'd spent the money on that sturdy dining room table. I climbed on top of her, her thighs opening in a succulent V as she clawed at my apron, lifting it, and groped after my cock in my dress slacks. I knelt over her as she eagerly undid my pants and took my cock into her mouth, her lips and tongue still warm from the salmon. She whimpered as her head bobbed up and down on me.

I guided her onto her back and slipped my body between her legs, her thighs closed tight around my hips. Pulling her thong to one side, I entered her, bringing a shudder to her body. I fucked her there on the table, slowly at first and then harder, course after course of deep thrusts into her, and when she came she clutched me so tight I couldn't resist it. I came inside her, my lips locked to hers, tasting oysters.

We had our dessert, after a fashion, sprawled in bed leaving stains everywhere. Who had the time to dab spilled wine and food from a body as luscious as that? I used my tongue instead, and cleanliness was not my first concern.

It's a tragedy, really. All that time spent whipping the chocolate mousse, preparing the violet sauce to drizzle in a suggestive snakelike S atop the firm skin of the chilled dessert. It's really a shame, all those aphrodisiacs in one dessert and she didn't even get to enjoy it...because she was too busy being fucked.

But now it's the morning, and she's sleeping contentedly, her breasts still rose-colored with crystallized red wine and her lips moist with other, more savory, liquors.

And morning's the best time for dessert.

Naked, I retrieve my apron and tie it around my body. I can feel my cock, wet with Iris's juices, rubbing against the rough cotton. The front of the apron is filthy, but isn't that what an apron's for? Ironically enough, this one didn't stop me from getting dirty last night.

I put the mousse on a tray and arrange it with a single violet blossom. I hear her sighing softly as I enter the bedroom.

THE SEX ALARM'S RINGING

12

Get Out of Bed

The bed has become a place of luxury to me! I would not exchange it for all the thrones in the world.

—Napoleon Bonaparte

Although Napoleon wanted nothing more than to be in his bed, I'm telling you to get out of yours! A change of scenery can make all the difference in enhancing your erotic experience. If you generally make love in the bedroom, why not move to the living room? Or the kitchen? Or the fire escape? How about doing it in front of a flickering fire, like in "Arran's Lure" by Saskia Walker:

Their kisses were raw, needy, while they stripped each other with eager hands. The first time was hard and fast, right there on the rug in front of the log fire. She welcomed the hard strength his body, hungry for it, her cunt hot and grabbing, holding him tight as he pulled back and lunged. As they got closer to the climax, he lifted up on his arms, looking down at her with searching eyes, and she latched her legs over his shoulders, sucking him ever deeper. The climax hit her in a dizzy, wild rush, and he followed fast, one hand pressing her pubic bone down onto his cock, the pressure releasing a second wave of pleasure through her.

Sex in the living room can be transcendent, as in Tyler Morgan's "Feng Shui Fuck":

She only seemed concerned with canoodling on the sofa with me—she was on one end, and I was on the other, and we overlapped in the most intricate ways. Each time she shifted, I learned new things about her body. And each time I moved, even slightly, she gave me a wicked encouraging smile. Until finally I reached over and took her glass of wine away, and then confiscated her cat-eye glasses, and began to unbutton her blouse.

She said nothing about the fact that I just threw her blouse to the floor, didn't pay attention to where her blouse wanted to be, or where my pants wanted to be. Soon she was naked. Just naked, beautiful naked, and I was naked, and we were fucking. Right there, on my leather sofa. Her lovely skin shining in the light, her hair long and loose, glasses off, pretty mouth on mine. I was so into her, hands roaming over her skin, bodies pressed together; moving her when I needed to get in her from behind, her ass against me, her breathing speeding up as I drove in deep.

Or make your sex dirty and clean at the same time, by hitting the shower, as in Shanna Germain's "Squeaky Clean":

You close your eyes while you wash, imagining your hand around your lover's shaft in the shower, water raining on you both. Your hands soaped and slippery, sliding down and back up to circle the tip until he thrusts his hips against your curled fist.

Sex on the floor has never sounded quite so delicious as in Helena Black's "Pink":

From his place facedown on the floor, all he can see are her legs, the shimmery pink of her stockings, the dark shadows where the polish on her toenails peeks through. His hands want to travel the length of those stockings, higher and higher, moving against the softness of material on flesh. He can imagine his fingers creeping up her slender legs, tracing their way around that lacy rim snuggled tight against her pale thighs.

Or as hardcore as being punished on an outdoor balcony in my story "Alone":

When the glass door slid open, I stayed prone, head down, until I felt Jack's hand on the top of my head. He stroked my hair, he petted me softly, gently. "Good girl," he murmured, his voice just reaching my ears. "Good girl."

And then he pulled me to standing, and wrapped me in his arms, and I could feel the softness of his shirt, and the rough fabric of his slacks, and the way his cool silver belt buckle pressed against me. The shudders working through my body came from a different reason now. Relief flooded me, and I would have wet his shirt with my tears, if he hadn't spun me around, so that I was looking back out on Sunset once more.

I truly do practice what I preach. Aside from sleeping, Sam and I may have used our mattress twice in all our years together. Crazy? Maybe. But true. We fuck in the kitchen, bathroom, living room, dining room, car. And you know what? If we've been to your house, we've probably fucked there.

This fact only occurred to me as I was writing this book, and I had to double-check with my man to make sure I wasn't exaggerating.

"It's surreal," he agreed. "Even after all this time, I can fuck you like I don't even know you. Fuck you like we just met."

Is that why people don't stay together? They lose that just-met-and-fucked feeling? Because I thought only I did that. Met someone, fell into bed right away, developed a hardcore relationship based on first-time fucking. When I was younger, I could be wilder with someone I didn't know than with someone I did. But now? Now, the two of us fuck like strangers all the time. (I'm scared that I'm stealing from a Kid Rock song here. So let me make this clear: Any resemblance to "So Hot" is purely unintentional. Because this is the basis not just for this entire book, but for my entire sex life.)

My advice, of course, is not for you to minutely change your routine so that you're ever so slightly different in bed. *Oooh, I have red socks on today. That's different from missionary, lights out, blue socks yesterday.*

My idea, my belief, my religion is that sex shouldn't get old, even as your relationship grows older—or *especially* as your relationship grows older. But I have to say something else. That fell-into-bed-right-away situation I mentioned above doesn't exactly describe us.

Yes, we fucked the first day we met.

But we didn't fuck in bed. We were outside, in a park in Berkeley, and I still have my torn stockings as souvenirs. Since then, Sam and I have proven again and again that the places you can make love in are limitless. Christen every room in your house, then move on to the neighbors'.

BANANA AFTERNOON

Jolene Hui

I was flipping through my recipe box when I found it—the perfect recipe. My mother's banana cake recipe was my favorite recipe of all time. I used to make this cake at least twice a year—leaving my bananas to ripen until they attracted fruit flies. After they were perfectly ripened, I'd carefully mash them in a dish, the scent filling my nostrils. The smell reminded me of summer and winter all wrapped into one. I could almost picture myself prancing around in my mom's kitchen in my old red bikini with the smell of banana cake in my nostrils. Making this cake was the only real time I ever could relax in the kitchen. And I hadn't done it in so long.

The day I rediscovered the recipe I was wandering around without a bra because of the hot summer weather. I needed to wear next to nothing to survive in the 105-degree heat. It was a Sunday, a perfect day for baking, and I didn't have air-conditioning. The sun was seeping through my screens, attacking everything in its path. The sweat dripped down my forehead as

I closed the recipe box and walked over to the kitchen counter. Setting the card down, I heard a noise in the other room. Marcus was taking a nap. He'd had a long night. As a musician, he often had gigs that lasted until the early morning. It was noon when I began to cook. I could hear him rustling the covers.

I climbed up onto the counter to sort through my cake pans. I wasn't sure what one I wanted exactly. I had inherited a variety of pans from my mother. I tried to be quiet as I clanked through all the pans, but I knew I was making too much noise. Marcus would awaken at any second and wonder what was going on.

As the oven preheated I started to sweat even more and the curls from my long black ponytail stuck to my moist neck. I had always cleaned the house naked and the heat was so unbearable now it was time to experiment with nude cooking. I stripped off my white tank top and little cotton shorts and was left with my favorite panties, white lace with little black bows along the top border.

My theory that I was being too loud was confirmed as I heard Marcus awaken and slam the bathroom door while I was humming and mixing in the baking powder. I sipped my iced tea and continued my mixing. My entire kitchen felt like the center of the sun as the oven heated up, anxiously waiting for the cake to be inserted into its hot center.

"What are you doing in there?" Five minutes after entering the bathroom, Marcus stepped out clad in a fluffy green bath towel. His semilong blond hair dripped onto the floor.

"Baking, why?" I bent over, ass up in the air, and picked up a piece of banana that had fallen to the floor.

"Ahhh," Marcus said, still standing in the same spot. "Can I watch you?"

I sucked the banana off my finger as I stared at his damp face. "Yeah, sure, why not?"

The cake batter smelled good as I finished mixing it. "Shit, I forgot to flour the pan!"

Marcus was now sitting in his towel on a bar stool in the doorway of the kitchen. "Why don't you just make cupcakes?" he asked, shrugging his shoulders.

"You're a genius," I said as I climbed back onto the counter to dig through my pans once again. I could smell Marcus sitting on the stool. He had just shaved and his aftershave was floating around the kitchen, up my nostrils and into my little bow-trimmed undies. The flour I had carelessly spilled on the countertop stuck to my shins as I dug through the pans. The sweat had made my body sticky and the flour was clinging and hardening on my damp legs.

"Eureka!" I yelled as I found my two cupcake tins. I couldn't even remember the last time I had used them.

Lining the tins with multicolored paper cups, I asked Marcus about his gig. "So, did you have groupies all over you last night?"

"Of course," he answered. "Would you expect anything less?"

"Oh shut the hell up," I said, finishing up with a blue paper cup.

"No, there weren't many groupies there," he said, "and I only thought about your sweet ass all night." Marcus ran his fingers through his hair and wiped his hand on his towel.

"Why don't you take your towel off?" I asked him as I spooned the batter into the cups.

"Just because you're naked doesn't mean I wanna strip down completely," he said, smiling. His eyes lit up as he stood and folded his arms across his chest.

My eyes shifted down as his towel loosened and fell to the floor.

"Join the club," I said as I sucked the batter off of my fingertips, one by one.

I finished filling the paper cups and put the pans into the steaming oven. They had to cook for twenty minutes—no more, no less. I carefully adjusted the timer. I would be devastated if my cupcakes didn't turn out perfectly. When I started to clean the counter, I heard Marcus approaching. He put his arms around my waist as I wiped down the bits of flour, sugar, and banana from the tile. I turned the water on and filled the mixing bowl as Marcus ran his fingers up and down my sides, tingles of pleasure ripping through my body. I grabbed the sponge and started to rinse all the spoons as his fingertips grazed my bare back and went down to the white lace panties I loved so much. My back arched and I moaned as he grabbed my ass and began to lick the sweat off my neck.

"Mmmm," I said softly. "I'm trying to clean up."

"So am I," he said as he hooked his fingers into my panties and slid them down to the floor.

I moaned and switched the water off. I felt his warmth on me as his fingers found their way to the front of my body. The scent of his clean hair and aftershave filled my pores as he stroked my wet center. I turned around and faced him quickly, my lips meshing with his, the batter on my lips rubbing all over his freshly shaved face. His hands moved quickly to my hips and he placed me on the freshly wiped countertop. I ran my fingers through his hair—the smell of baking banana cupcakes heavy in the thick air. I had accidentally decorated my chest with batter as I was spooning it into the pans, but Marcus quickly helped clean me off with his hot and able tongue. I spread my legs as I felt his throbbing cock getting closer and closer to me. I shrieked with delight as he finally shoved it in and my body slightly slipped toward him on the moist countertop. I breathed in soft quick breaths as he cleaned the batter off my body and expertly slid in and out.

When it started to get too slippery, he pulled out of me and helped me off the counter. He turned me around and began to kiss my back while pushing me slowly to the ground, my back still to him. After adjusting my body, he found his way inside me once again, sliding in and out of me while my hands were immersed in the cupcake ingredients on the floor. He leaned over me and I felt his hair grazing my shoulders. His tongue on my ear, I screamed with pleasure as the ripples ran through my body. He went on pumping until I felt him burst inside me, his voice moaning in my ear.

We collapsed to the floor as the buzzer went off on the oven. Still breathing heavily, I left Marcus on the floor and stood up suddenly. I didn't want my cupcakes to burn. Grabbing my two favorite plaid oven mitts, I removed the freshly baked cakes from the oven and placed them on top of my stove.

Marcus was still on the floor when I took off my oven mitts and went to the pantry to retrieve the items for the frosting.

"You never give up, do you?" he asked, sitting up, his right arm covered in flour.

"I have to start making the frosting," I said, feeling his come running along my right leg. I reached down, wiped it off with my index finger and sucked it off as he stared at me, desire showing in his eyes. I broke the staring contest with Marcus and gazed into the pantry, taking inventory of what I needed.

"These cupcakes better be damn good," said Marcus, lying back down on the floor, not caring that he was slathered in all of the cupcake ingredients.

"Of course they are," I answered, offended. "I wouldn't be making them if they were gross."

I grabbed a clean mixing bowl from the bottom shelf and began adding ingredients. It was a simple frosting, with powdered sugar, melted butter, and vanilla. Marcus yelled at me from the floor, "I think you should come back down here."

I ignored him as I vigorously whipped the frosting.

"Ally, I think you should come back down here."

I felt the sweat starting to form again on my forehead and my upper body. I knew this recipe by heart and decided to make a little extra as a surprise for Marcus, who was still on the floor, begging me to come back. The cupcakes would take quite some time to cool off so I took two full handfuls of frosting and turned toward Marcus.

"What are you going to do with those?" he asked, a huge smile creeping across his face.

"What do you think I'm going to do?" I questioned him back as I walked to him, hands still full of the frosting. "You know this is pretty much just sugar, right?"

"I know what it is." Marcus put his hands behind his head and stretched his legs out.

I knelt down to him and put one handful of frosting on his stomach. He shrieked at the stickiness of it. "What are you going to do with that other handful?"

"Give me your hand and you decide what you want to do with it," I responded.

He stuck out his hand and I gave him a chunk of the sugary frosting.

"My turn first," I said as I started rubbing the frosting all over his body. My tongue began to lick it all off and I could feel Marcus twitching with pleasure. I licked his stomach and his shoulders, my saliva leaving trails on his skin. I worked my way down to his lower stomach and when I got to his cock, it was already throbbing and hard. I placed my mouth around it and thoroughly cleaned it off, sucking and licking as necessary. When I was finished, Marcus rubbed his frosting on the floor, rolled on top of me and entered me with lightning speed. He stuck his tongue in my mouth, tasting all the frosting I'd just licked off his body. I moaned as he plunged harder and faster, running his frosting laced fingers through my hair and tugging on it as he came closer to coming. I was aware of the pile of frosting on the ground and took it in my left hand, slathering it the best that I could across my chest. I pushed away from him, rolled him over onto his back, and got on top of him, my frosted tits in his face. He gratefully sucked and licked them as I moved my hips up and down on his. With an iced thumb, Marcus rubbed my clit and I groaned with pleasure, exploding all over him, lost as he moaned and came inside me.

As we reclined on the floor and stared at the ceiling, we were aware that Marcus would need to take another shower and that I definitely needed to frost the cupcakes before the frosting dried out. Slowly standing up, I made my way to the countertop and gave the frosting a quick stir before I carefully frosted all of the twenty-four perfect banana cupcakes. I handed one to Marcus who had gotten to his feet by that time. We looked at each other and laughed at each other's icing flecked body hair and when I finally bit into a cupcake, I was so overcome with joy I didn't mind that the leftover chunks of icing on my body had begun to melt in the sun. That cupcake was the most heavenly thing I'd tasted all day.

Well, almost.

13 | THREE IMPORTANT WORDS

Location, Location, Location

Nature is by and large to be found out of doors,
a location where, it cannot be argued, there are
never enough comfortable chairs.
—Fran Lebowitz

You've left the safe haven of your bedroom. In fact, you've made love in the living room and the dining room, the bathroom and the kitchen. If you live on the East Coast, you've done it in the clubbed basement, you lucky fucking people. (Where's *my* clubbed basement?) If you live on the West Coast, you've done it with the windows open in the middle of December. (Take that, East Coasters!)

Now's the time to ratchet up the stakes. Open your front door and look outside. It's a big, big world out there, with so many places to play. (Good thing you don't need a lot of comfortable chairs when you're having super-hot sex!) In fact, sometimes the world may seem too big. I mean, where does one start?

Well, why not right out there on the lawn, as the characters do in Stephen D. Rogers' "Flashers":

She stepped from behind a tree and flashed him.

He flashed her from behind a trellis.

Their bare skin glowed in short bursts, like two fireflies dancing around each other until darkness fell and the two lovers finally met and joined on a bed of soft grass.

Or in a nearby park, like in "Wet" by Mathilde Madden:

I slide my hands around and down the back of his jeans, grabbing his arse like I wanted to do in the pub. It's even better than I imagined. High and firm and...oh god, I want to see him naked. I want to taste him. Press my mouth on him. Feel his skin, his heat, his delicious need.

Twisting the two of us around, so he's the one with his back pressed against the tree trunk, I bring my hands round to the front of his jeans and start to undo them. It takes forever. What he's still doing to my neck makes it hard to concentrate. But I manage. I get his jeans off. And his underwear. His cock springs into my hands, hard and unnaturally warm in the damp night air. I press close to him so he can rub against my leg. He moans deep in his throat and I gasp.

I untangle myself from him and slide onto my knees in the mud. The ground is cold, but my desire and the heat pulsing from his body keeps me warm. His cock is damp with precome, a little droplet on the tip, sparkling in the moonlight, just like the glittering raindrops earlier.

I'd love to find an elevator like the one in Sommer Marsden's "A Smear of Red":

He turned to her. "You know in most buildings you can't stop the elevator. Not nowadays. It has an emergency shutoff but it can't be done manually anymore." He reached out and traced one pearl button on her blouse. "Probably to prevent the kind of things that are about to happen in this elevator." One finger dipped below her collar, tracing a tiny expanse of lace.

Her nipples peaked instantly. That was it. Right there. The feeling that she lived for. Feeling alive and electrified and hungry. Angela bit her lip a little too hard, trying to focus.

"I'm glad that our company is too cheap to update our elevator," she whispered.

The dance club in D. L. King's "Hard Wet Silk" is a completely unexpected location, especially for the man:

I didn't say anything. We'd been dancing—grinding against each other on the couple of crowded square feet that passed for a dance floor. It was one of those new, trendy Brooklyn bars. All the hipsters flooded in these days because Brooklyn was hot. Well, Brooklyn seemed pretty much like Brooklyn to me except now it was more expensive, although still cheap by Manhattan standards.

I'd maneuvered him into a darkish corner, his back up against the wall.

"No, really…" he laughed. It was nervous laughter.

I licked my lips.

"I can't just get…I mean…there are people here…someone will see…" He looked around me, as if to make sure he was right and people were really watching him. I stood there, blocking his path, blocking the view. I calmly tilted my head and looked at his face.

Craig J. Sorensen's "Never a Rookie" explores BDSM sex in a restaurant walk-in:

She gripped his chin in her talon hand. "No two ways about it, you need to be punished."

Phillip's heart fluttered. He gulped a breath. Liz watched his face closely. Her hand began to release.

"Uh, yes—mistress?"

She nodded and stiffly slapped his cheek. "Stand up."

Phillip complied. She sat on the box and took his Michelob. She drew a long drink while she untied his apron with the other hand. The apron fell to the cold floor. She stroked the large bulge at the front of his jeans. Phillip's hands instinctively moved toward his crotch.

"Hands on your head!"

Saskia Walker dives sensually into sex in a pool in "A Quick Dip":

He stroked her inner thighs and she moaned in response. His chest rode up against her pussy. He felt her flesh slide down his body as he stood up, her shaved pussy coming to rest low on his abdomen. His cock bounced up eagerly under her.

She drew in a lingering breath when his body applied pressure between her thighs. Her breasts bobbed in the water. He stroked them, his fingertips exploring the peaks of her nipples. He glanced down at the juncture of their bodies, wanting to push his cock home, but wanting to know how much she wanted it first. He thrust a finger inside her. She began to quiver and her arms grew rigid. The water in the pool began to lap over her body as she twisted with pleasure.

Marilyn Jaye Lewis checks into a cheap motel in "Dinner at Eight":

My soaking pussy meets the blanket and I wonder how many other slick cunts have wiped against it over the years. It doesn't matter. Right at this moment, I couldn't care less about anybody's slick cunt but my own. Now my acute sense of hearing is my lifeline to the entire world. I am only a waiting mouth, a clit, and two very eager holes. And for some reason, as the wine and hormones battle for supremacy in my veins, I feel absolutely alive. Following the mystery of this man is now my only goal.

Then there's one of my all-time favorite stories, "Selling Point" by Carl Kennedy, which takes place in the S/M dungeon of a house that's for sale. Remember those three words— location, location, location:

I nudged the skirt with my toe. Michelle stepped out of it and I kicked the garment across the room.

I went to the cabinet and selected a paddle. Michelle's eyes were wide as she watched me return to her.

I bent down and took hold of her ankles. Michelle did not resist as I fitted her ankles into the padded metal of the St. Andrew's cross's built-in manacles. I could hear her breath, mingling with the hum of the heater.

"Are you warm enough?"

"Yes," she said softly. "Quite."

When I had her restrained, I ran the paddle up the back of her bare thighs and slipped it under the waistband of her panties. She squirmed.

"This certainly is a selling point," I said, and spanked her.

For me, doing it in a bathroom never gets old. I've written about a frisky threeway between two Frankenfurters and one Brad in a movie theater bathroom in "Melt with You," and about raw sex in a restaurant bathroom in "When You Say You Love Me":

He doesn't say another word then. He just grabs me by the arm—oh, I love when he grabs me by the arm—and he takes me with him up the steep set of stairs to one of the two unisex bathrooms at the top. The door doesn't close all the way. There is a hook-eye latch that leaves a half inch of space all around. Anyone waiting for the restroom would be able to see inside, to easily hear the next words he says:

"Hands on the wall."

The plaster is covered all over with names and numbers, with graffiti that's been here since I was in high school.

Why? Why did I go to Villains? I could have come directly from Wasteland, could have skipped Aardvarks.

I do what he says with a sigh he doesn't appreciate. He expects my obedience without attitude. This is something I can't always give.

He flips up the dress, runs his hands over my fishnets before tearing them down. He spanks me with his hand on my panty-clad ass, until I stop worrying about what I should have done. What I might have done. And start worrying about what he's going to do. What I hope he'll do.

Worry and hope. Yeah, they go together. They go together in times like this.

I worry that he's going to take my panties down. That he's going to use his belt on me. Here, in a public place, where any noise will carry.

And, truthfully? I worry that he won't.

I look down at my glossy blue Docs. I look down as he slips my panties down my thighs. I look down at the navy against cobalt, the satin against leather, and I suck in my breath as I hear the sound of his buckle.

It's leather on skin then, the sound and the sensation. It's graffiti through the blur of my tears, as he makes me count. As I try to keep up.

He smacks my ass and my upper thighs, pushes down on the lower part of my back so that I give him the arch he wants.

There are footsteps on the stairs, then. Are we found out? No. An unseen customer takes the second bathroom, and he continues to thrash me in that hypnotic rhythm. Until the blue at my feet is one azure blur, and he puts one hand in front of my body, strokes my clit to make me come.

And it's blue. I swear. The sparks in my eyes. The incandes-

*cent light that fills my head. That neon glow. The cold ever-
lasting fire. It's blue.*

God, yes, bathrooms really do work for me.

But these are only the tiniest sample of the kinds of places
you might play. Swimming pools, rec rooms, bars, dressing
rooms…it's up to you to find the location (location, location)
that makes your heart skip a beat. And won't you ever have a
blast looking!

EROTIC FICTION

FRUITS OF THE FOREST

Kristina Lloyd

The woodland edge was tangled with great loops of wild clematis, and underfoot lay another tangle of barbed wire and brambles. I was slightly drunk so I placed my feet carefully, tramping on barbs with thick-soled gardening boots, holding my dress high so it wouldn't get snagged.

Oh, follow me, I thought. *Please follow me.* I was horny from sunshine and wine, and from the way he'd ignored me from the moment I arrived. When he plays hard to get, I'm the easiest girl in town.

Behind me lay the community garden, a jungle of bean wigwams, tumbledown sheds, orange flares of nasturtium, and huge sleepy sunflowers on a slope of land by the old railway track. I glanced back and through the trees and could see people milling about, smoke from the barbecue rising above the greenery like mists from a primeval swamp.

No one was following, so I stumbled on, taking my time because I was eager to get caught. The forest floor crackled and snapped, and around me trees grew taller and thicker. I was hot and thirsty, and the filtered leafy sunlight was a highball tumbler of lime juice I couldn't drink. Birds twittered somewhere unseen, and I began to feel spooked and lonely. Perhaps I should have told someone where I was going. But no, he'd seen me leave, hadn't he? I'd thrown him my best flirty glance and he'd responded with a quick, tilted smile. Based on past experience, I'd have sworn a smile like that meant "I want to fuck you to high heaven." So why the delay? What was he doing? Grilling a burger?

I paused by some scrawny bushes to text him, thumbing in those three little words: *tight white pantie—*

But I didn't complete my message. A flurry of noise behind me made my heart speed up, and I spun around, phone falling to the ground as a body thumped up hard against mine. I didn't even get chance to scream. A hand was clamped over my mouth before I'd barely drawn breath. The hand wore a black leather glove and the smell of it was strong beneath my nostrils: an animal scent with a hint of manufacture. It added a squalid urbanity to the forest aromas of earthiness, wood rot, foxes and wild garlic. That hand didn't belong here. It was cruel and cold, and it belonged to alleyways and authority.

At the time, however, I wasn't thinking this. I was fighting and clawing, squealing in protest and thinking, *What the fuck?*

Together, we stumbled down a rugged incline to a small clearing. My heart was going nineteen to the dozen, my breath rushing against the leather in a humid pump and suck.

"Don't scream," he warned gently, and his voice wasn't the one I'd been hoping for.

He backed me up against a tree, uncovering my mouth as he moved behind the trunk to catch at my wrists. I didn't scream. I just breathed hard and fast, glimpsing a skinny figure in jeans, trainers and a hooded top. A length of thin rope flicked in the corner of my eye—hemp twine from the garden—and then he was using it to tether my wrists behind the tree trunk. The bark was rough on my bare arms, and my skin was clammy. No, it wasn't who I was expecting, that was for sure.

He crouched at my feet where the ground was lumpy with roots and looped the cord above my chunky boot. A small backpack lay in front of us but that didn't give me much of a clue.

"Danny?" I asked, but got no reply. He was intent on securing me, bunny-hopping around the tree base with the rope. In the distance a bird cawed noisily, a jay or magpie. When it stopped, the silence was eerie. Something rustled in the undergrowth nearby. The man passed the rope behind the trunk then caught my other leg in another loop. His gloved hand brushed against my shins, and the touch of it lingered. As I watched him work, carefully shielding his face, those dark anonymous hands took on a life of their own. I could imagine them in all sorts of places: on the wheel of a car, in the pockets of a cashmere coat, on a pallbearer's hands, forcing the lock of a lamplit door. They were like puppets, dancing and disembodied.

His hands must have been hot. My feet certainly were. I wished I'd worn pretty sandals so my toes could breathe. But the garden terrain was tricky, and I like to be able to move about freely. Ironic, considering I was now tied to a tree.

From behind, the man reached around and let his leather fingers drift briefly over my face. I could hear him breathing from his exertions, and my own breath was choppy too.

"Mike?" I tried, and I heard him laugh. If this wasn't a man I knew, I was in big trouble.

He stepped out into the clearing, shucking off his zip-up top and stooping for his bag. Tall, angular, with sinewy arms, wearing a faded black T-shirt, he had scruffy peroxide spikes and some serious cheekbones. "My god, Brett?! Is that right? Is that your name?"

He turned, grinning with sly confidence and scattering half-glances in my direction. Stubble speckled his jaw, and his dark brows matched the dark deliberate roots peeping through the bleach. He looked as if he'd been up all night, half-angel, half-devil, a wasted, fucked-up pretty boy.

I glanced away. On the edge of the clearing, a haze of midges shimmered in sunlight. The tree trunk felt thick against my open thighs. The woodland was still and tranquil. Brett took a large margarine tub from his backpack and peeled off the top. Inside were raspberries. My mouth watered: pimply scarlet berries, fuzzed with hair, flecked with leaf, and lying several cushiony inches deep.

"I want to feed you," he said, stepping closer. "I've always wanted to feed you."

Lust thumped me open because I'd no idea that this man had wanted to *anything* me. I watched his black leather fingertips scoop up a little cluster of fruit. Thin juices bled from them as he stepped closer still, and a drip fell as he brought the berries to my mouth. I was so thirsty, and the raspberries crumbled on my tongue, a brush of fur popping to sharp wet sweetness and then, too quickly, they slid down my throat. The insides of my cheeks tingled.

"More," I said, and he fingered up another serving, hurrying them to my lips. Juice dribbled on my chin, and I snatched a suck on his leather fingers when they were deep in my mouth. God, what a combination. Flavors burst, and it all tasted of summer and peaty bonfires with the slightest tang of licorice and metal. Those berries couldn't get any riper. They were at their limit, on the edge of decay and close to collapse.

So was I. Brett: I hardly knew him. A friend of a friend, a man

I'd probably chatted with once or twice while privately admiring his cheekbones. He'd been at the barbecue but we hadn't even said hi. And here he was, ladling raspberries into my mouth, allowing me to suck on his leather gloves as if tart sweet fluid might ooze from his fingers.

Before I could swallow, he pressed more raspberries into my mouth then squashed several onto the flat of my chest, rubbing with his gloved hand. Cool juice trickled toward my cleavage, and my skin was smeared with smashed fruit.

"Don't waste them," I said, pulling against my ropes and opening wide for more.

"Not going to," he replied, and he set down the punnet and lifted the hem of my dress.

He twisted the fabric tight, wringing it into a tail which he tucked behind me, leaving me exposed from the waist downward. He stooped for more raspberries, then, pulling the elastic, he slid his hand into those tight white panties and crushed soft red berries into my cunt. His leather fingers paddled and probed, mashing me and the fruit into one glorious pulpy crimson mess.

I groaned, wanting to slide down the tree in mindless, soporific lust. He took more berries, pushing them higher into me this time, his hard, leathered fingers stirring in my hole. I felt like I was part of a recipe: *insert fruit and mix well*. Around us, trees whispered in the breeze, a bee buzzed somewhere at ground level, and I could feel my face flushing with shame and arousal.

Brett watched me, his blue-gray eyes shy and fascinated. "Is it good?" he smiled, fingers still working.

I could barely speak. "Fuck, yes," I breathed. "So good...it's so good."

As I moved, the bark scoured the backs of my thighs and

arms, and the twine rubbed my wrists and shins. But I couldn't keep still. Brett's fingers squirmed. *I* squirmed. He shuffled closer, resting his free hand against the trunk and leaning toward my mouth. A glint of sunlight sparked on his dark lashes and his breath was warm against my skin. Carefully, he took my lower lip between his teeth, pulling ever so gently. He repeated the action, teeth lightly scraping, and all the while his gloved hand kept churning between my thighs. I whimpered, trying to kiss him back, but he dodged my mouth, smearing kisses over my face instead, bristles scratching.

His words blurred against my skin. "I've always wanted to feed you. Feed you. And feed me." Kiss, kiss, went his lips. "Here. Try."

He withdrew his hand from me and brought it up to my mouth. The glove was hot and moist, and he held a finger sidelong to my lips. I licked through my fast-rushing breath, and so did he. I tasted myself, all mixed up with raspberries and leather. And I tasted him, the quick lash of his tongue and his cool, clean saliva. Between my thighs, I was hot and syrupy, damp white cotton holding a pouch of pulped raspberries. He rubbed me there, and his breath tickled my ear as he murmured, "And now I'm going to gobble you up."

My head spun as he dropped to his knees. Leather fingers brushed my thighs and he pulled down my underwear as far as it would go. I strained against my bondage, thrusting forward, hips trying to seek him out. For a moment, the forest air breezed against my bared pussy and then his mouth was on me, hot, sodden and writhing.

I moaned loudly, the sound seeming to shock the clearing where only birds and bees made noises. He gulped me down, tongue and lips searching out fruit and flesh. My clit was a raspberry that wouldn't dissolve but he tried his damnedest, licking, sucking, flicking, rocking. His hands made sticky prints on my thighs where he gripped me, and he nuzzled deep, all greedy, slurpy and shameless. When he drove those strong leather fingers up inside me, I came hard, spilling fruit and nectar into his hungry, wolfish throat. The trees whirled in a haze of sunny greens, my body clenched, my cunt melted and the bees just kept on bumbling and buzzing.

Brett stood, his chin and mouth glistening with pinkish stains and crimson gobbets. He looked like he'd been feeding at a trough. He wiped the back of his hand across his mouth and grinned.

"One day..." he said, looking more satisfied than perhaps he ought. He nodded in the direction we'd both come from. Somewhere beyond the woods there was a party going on. "I've got to get back," he said, slinging his bag onto his shoulder.

"What about me?" I said, but he was already off, scrambling up the slope he'd dragged me down not long ago.

Was he going to leave me here? Pinned open like a butterfly, gummy, half-naked and defenseless against wasps?

"Hey!" I shouted.

He paused at the top of the slope, casting around on the forest floor.

"My phone!" I hollered, remembering that I'd dropped it. He'd obviously remembered too because he pounced for it before my words were finished. I could see him looking at the screen, and I recalled my text: *tight white pantie–*

"*S!*" I called. "Needs an *s* on the end!"

He pressed a button.

"Is it for Tom?" he asked.

"Well, who else?" I replied.

He thumbed a few buttons and, from the smile on his face, I could tell the text was sent.

He tossed the phone to the ground. "If I pass him en route," he said, walking away, "I'll tell him where you are."

I struggled against my ropes. "Strawberries!" I yelled. "Tell him to bring strawberries!"

He turned to grin and I knew, without a doubt, that the two men would pass.

PLANES, TRAINS, AND AUTOMOBILES

14

Take This Show on the Road

For my part, I travel not to go anywhere, but to go. I travel for travel's sake. The great affair is to move.

—Robert Louis Stevenson

Forget lions and tigers and bears—oh, my—and consider buses and trains and taxis—*ohhhh*, my. Sex in vehicles can max out so many different types of turn-ons. For exhibitionists, there's the thrill of potentially being seen. Cars often bring back memories of yesterday's make-out sessions. And personally I find travel sexy in general, so screwing in a vehicle comes naturally. I've written about sex on a cable car ("I Left My Thong in San Francisco") and sex in the Eurotunnel ("Chunnel of Love"), and I did the research for both of those stories to give them that extra realistic quality.

What's so exciting to me is the sheer number of

transportation devices to fuck in—I mean choose from—I mean, well, *both*.

There's sex in a ski lift in Cheyenne Blue's "White Rush":

"In a gondola, yes." Neil's eyes twinkled with the adrenaline-white rush that skiing always brings. "As long as it's far enough. I've done it on the gondola at Whistler—that's ten kilometers long."

"No gondolas here," I pointed out. "Just the four-chair lifts. You couldn't do it without freezing your butt. And how would you get into position anyway?"

He thought for a moment, absently burrowing his fingers under my thermals to the warm skin beneath. His fingers were icy from the pint he'd been holding and the residual bone-deep chill of the mountain air. "You'd have to have the bar up to kneel on the seat, and hope you didn't fall off twisting around."

And sex after a motorcycle ride in my story "Leather and Lace":

My favorite experience with her so far, my most memorable time, was when she took me riding with her, on the back of the bike, and drove us to a secluded spot outside of town. I think she'd scoped it out on one of her solo rides. When we parked, my pussy was drenched from the vibrations of the motorcycle. I had almost come simply from sitting on the seat and grabbing her tightly around the waist.

Thomas S. Roche tackled sex in a taxi (with the driver watching) in "Operator 84":

Your lacy thong comes smoothly down your thighs, over your ankles. You kick off your flats and tuck your panties into the pocket of my dress slacks.

"Lots of great dancing down in Tribeca nowadays," says the cabdriver, looking at me in the rearview mirror. I can see the side of her face and she's smiling; she's got a bright, enticing smile,

and I spend about five seconds trying to figure out whether she knows what's going on. "Yup, the neighborhood's really bouncing back."

"Uh-huh," I say as you reach for my cock. "Bouncing."

By then you've slid down behind the seat and you're kneeling between my legs. Knowing better than to argue with you, of course, I spread them enough to give you access.

"Yeah," I say, my breath coming short as your hand closes around the rapidly growing bulge in my pants. "There's nothing quite as great as a night dancing." I swallow nervously as you make short work of my belt and pants, apparently not caring if the driver recognizes the telltale jingle of my belt buckle, the revealing sound of my zipper going down.

H. L. Berry's "The Train Terminates Here" doesn't simply feature sex on any train; this superhot story features sex on the *Flying Scotsman!*

She dropped to her knees and unzipped his trousers. "What do you think?"

"In the loo?"

She looked around. "It's not so bad. They keep them spotlessly clean these days, and this one is extralarge, so you can get a wheelchair in."

"We're going to do it in the disabled toilet of the Flying Scotsman?*"*

Victoria reached into his trousers and pulled out his cock. "Yes. We are."

The interminable trip to Las Vegas will never seem the same to you after reading Kis Lee's scorching "Bus Ride":

He moved his hand from my thigh to my forearm, lightly brushing my bare skin with his fingertips. His touch went from the inside of my wrist to my elbow and up toward my bicep, stroking my skin slowly like he was remembering my texture. I

watched his gaze slide over my breasts, my stomach, and lower.
When the bus rolled into motion, I jumped. I hadn't even
heard the driver announce our departure. Shifting in my seat, I
noticed that all the passengers had congregated around the front
and middle. A few middle-aged ladies were discussing which
casino had the best buffet.
"No one can see us," Dave whispered.

Mike Kimera's "Have a Nice Day" details ultradecadent sex
in a limo. *No Way Out's* got nothing on Kimera:

She makes a call on her cell phone and a white stretch limo
pulls up. She leads you to the limo by the hand. You worry about
getting in without flashing your dildo-filled cunt at the world.
People know you here. She solves the problem for you. Once the
door is open, she pushes you hard on the back of the head and
you fall into the limo face first, ass in the air. As you scramble for
balance you hear the sound of yourself coming. The video in the
limo shows you being fucked by me and coming hard.

But even if you can't try your luck in a local limo, tryst in a
taxi, or fuck on the *Flying Scotsman,* an everyday automobile
will work just fine as evidenced in Sommer Marsden's "Risk":

His hands pinned my hips as he walked me back slowly. Soon
my back was pressed against the cold, red steel, the door handle
jabbing me lower down. The cold air froze in my throat and I
made a small, wounded sound. A needy sound. The feel of his
hands on me was dark and sinister, secretly pleasing.

"So you want to risk it? The lives we know? The lives of
others? Is that what you're telling me? You're willing to possibly
throw it all away just to fuck in the back of my car?"

"To fuck you in the back of your car," I answered, forcing
way more bravado into my voice than I felt. "Yes."

Or on the hood of a car, like in James Walton Langolf's
"Abraham":

He holds her still, his cock raw and burning, near to bursting inside of her. When she opens her eyes, the steel has softened to the silvery gray of sunlit water and her mascara has smudged prettily across her cheek. She puts her lips against his. It isn't a kiss but something else and she breathes out, taking him still deeper inside and he whispers her own name back to her.

When he lays her back on the hood of the car again he's careful to hold her head. He's slamming into her and the hood ornament is digging a hole in his thigh. The rain streams off his skin and she's saying something but he can't hear the words over the rolling thunder or the ocean sound of his own beating blood. When he comes, it feels like something inside him is tearing loose and whatever it is—poison or poetry—he wants to give it all to her, bury it deep inside where she can't dig it out.

And then there are fantastical vehicles, ones that don't exist in real life, but do exist in the brilliant minds of their creators. Like the bicycle with a dildo in N. T. Morley's "Sit-and-Spin":

Kasey climbed onto the machine and spread her pussy lips with her finger, positioning her tight opening at the head of the big cock. She winced as she sat down, feeling the enormous head stretch her in a way she'd never been stretched before. She let out a little yelp as the head popped into her, and another round of giggles went through the room. Kasey had to wriggle her body back and forth to force herself down the length of the shaft. When she finally sat atop the dildo, she could feel the head pushing into her cervix, the thick ridges near the base rubbing against her G-spot. Every movement she made brought a fresh pulse of heat to her body. She could feel her nipples stiffening with the stimulation.

Where do you go from here?

Brainstorm a list of vehicles you'd like to try (real or imaginary), and then cross off each one as you succeed. Choose normal ones, like Cadillac or pickup truck, or more difficult ones like a fire truck or unicycle. Or simply *imagine* being transported to ecstasy in each one. This is yet one more place where fantasy can sometimes take you farther than reality, without the chance of being ticketed for indecent exposure.

Of course, you could always *play* Good Cop/Naughty Speeder. Or *I* could. I wonder what I'd have to do for Sam to get out of a ticket...?

RED LIGHT, GREEN LIGHT

Alison Tyler

"R ed light," Molly announces gleefully, resting her hand on top of Jason's thigh and squeezing. He removes his tie and tosses it at her, and she giggles and uses it to pull her hair away from her face, knotting the expensive scarlet silk in a bow beneath her ebony mane.

How pretty she looks in the pale twilight, her face kissed with a fever-flush of excitement. He smiles at her, and nearly runs the red, but she stops him in time, saying, "Red light," and flicking her bangs out of her face with a triumphant little nod of her head—the same look she wears when she creams him at tennis. Jason unbuttons his blue shirt and pitches it into the backseat where it comes to rest on top of his loafers, belt, slacks, and socks. The only items of hers in the pile are a crocheted white sweater and her high-heeled sandals.

"Red light," she says. "Red light, Jas." He's already down to his striped boxers, still a good ten miles from home. But now his luck changes. They zip through two greens in a row, and

Molly, giving him the sweetest smile ever, a light pink color to her cheeks, takes off her white thigh-high fishnets, one at a time, and adds them to the pile. Jason speeds through a yellow—obviously hoping she'll remove the dress—but she calls "foul," and rightfully so.

There are rules to this game. Silly rules, admittedly, but rules nonetheless. It's a spicy, after-work game, a summer-night-on-the-way-home-from-a-show game, an anytime-day-or-night game, if you're in the mood. And the rules are as follows: Driver removes one article of clothing at every red light (full stops, only—if the light changes as the driver pulls up, it's the passenger's turn). Passenger removes an item of dress at each green light. It's safer that way, if you think about it.

But what happens when one of you is left without any more pieces to remove, and you're still miles from home? That, of course, is where the real fun begins.

"Foul," she pouts. "You cheated. Off with the boxers." He gives her a sly smile, wondering to himself, *Does she really think I mind losing this round?*

"Next stop," he says. "I can't take 'em off while I'm driving, you know."

"At the next light, Jas, you *owe* me. The boxers, plus..."

"Plus...?"

"I'm thinking." The light ahead turns amber, then crimson, and she blushes as she says, "Take them off, and kiss me *there* until the light changes."

There... His sweetheart, his darling Molly, so shy with the words, but so bold with her actions. She has a difficult time saying "pussy," would never say "cunt," can barely say "cock." Though it makes it that much more exciting for him when she does.

Jason plays fair, now, sliding out of his blue-and-white boxer shorts. As he removes them, Molly hits the RECLINE on her seat and he bends and buries his face under her dress. It's a long light, a three-way, and he has time to run his tongue the length of the seam of her panties, from the waistband down and up again, tasting her fragrant honey through the thin white cotton.

"Go," she whispers, and he sits back upright, a nude man tooling along in a black VW, grateful, not for the first time, that he doesn't drive a convertible. They make the next light, and Molly casually peels off her floral sundress. She's sitting at his side in a matching underwear set that he bought her for Valentine's Day: white bra and panties made of the sheerest cotton, trimmed in delicate eyelet lace. The car is filled with the scent of heat, the intoxicating perfume of her sex rising. The heady aroma makes him dizzy, near-desperate to stop at the next light so that he can taste her again. But he cruises through, despite slowing, and Molly, sitting up again, slides out of her bra. Her pert breasts are a wonder to see, the way they seem to perch on her slender frame, perfectly round and proud. The man in the next car can't take his eyes off them, either.

"Look at the road," she admonishes, and Jason works his best to follow her command, although he can't keep himself from snaking one hand out to touch her rose-petal skin, the softness of her creamy flesh amazing to him as always. How someone could be that soft, that supple, never ceases to astound him. To thrill him.

"Oh..." she starts, as he makes the next light, because now they're even. Her panties are at the floor by her feet. Her cheeks are the color of the sky outside, a summer palette of colors, ranging from pink to scarlet. She is lovely when she blushes.

"Call it," Jason says, watching the light ahead go red.

"No, wait." And she's right. This light is a quickie, and it turns green before they make it to the intersection. He putts through it, saying, "Down on me, girl, now," and she quickly obeys, moving her slender body in the seat to comfortably reach his cock, drinking him down her sweet throat and suckling. "Keep it going 'til the next light," he tells her, twisting one hand in her dark curls, stroking her naked back, casually losing his hands in the curves, the secret places of her body.

"Dmn't lmine…" she mumbles, her mouth filled with cock. But he speaks her language, knows what she's trying to say. She's warning him not to lie, and he won't. In order to trick her, he'd have to go through a red, and safety is important in this game. (Let this be a warning to all you lovers out there making mental notes: You don't want to be pulled over by a cop for reckless driving. Not with your I.D. in your wallet and your wallet in your slacks and your slacks in the backseat of the car.)

She feels him ease up on the gas and move to the brake, but it's only a stop sign, which doesn't count either way. You have to stop. There's no chance to it. No fun. They continue, nearing the residential area by the beach where they live, the streets well shaded with purple-blossomed jacaranda trees. There are only a few more lights until their turnoff. He misses the first one.

"My turn," she sighs. "Or rather, *your* turn."

He assumes the position, reaching over her to hit the lever that sends her seat back in the reclining position again. She giggles as he tickles her pussy with his tongue, then moans at the feel of his five o'clock shadow brushing the outer lips…then she sighs as he finds the right spot, the perfect spot, and begins to make those dizzyingly tight circles around her clit.

"Mmm," comes her dark moan, and the sound of her voice gone husky and whisper-soft works to excite him even more. He dips his tongue deeper inside her, going for the very source of her pleasure.

"Green," she sighs, stretching the word out as if it's some

kind of release, "Greeeeeennnn." He swallows hard, sits upright, and hits the gas, pulling into the intersection as the car horns behind him begin to blare. Molly stays in the same position, sprawled out in the passenger seat, one hand in her lap covering her nakedness, like Venus as she stepped free from the ocean, her hand so modestly in place.

He makes it through the next light, the last light, and without a word from him, Molly swivels around and takes up where she left off. Her mouth is hungry and open and willing on his cock. She takes him in deep, one of her little hands squeezing the base of his shaft, the other caressing his balls. What he wants most to do in this world is close his eyes and wrap his hands in her hair, letting her work him until she's finished.

But instead, he makes the left turn into their complex. In effect, it's still his turn because he won the last round. Molly blushes becomingly, waiting for his command. He could make her cross the parking lot to their apartment totally nude, if he wanted. He could hand her the keys and follow a few steps behind her, watching the pretty jiggle of her hips as she tried not to run.

He doesn't, though. Instead, he says, "Get back to work, darling," and he revs the engine, switches into reverse, and backs the car out of their space. She shoots him one puzzled glance, but doesn't question him, and in an instant he is back in heaven, with her head bobbing up and down between his legs.

"That's the girl, that's my sweetheart."

He drives down Seventh Street in Santa Monica, looking for a place to stop, and finds it, finally, a cul-de-sac off the road, in one of the unknown pockets of wealth. There are no sidewalks here, just huge houses surrounded by acres of trees. He misses the second to last light, and at Molly's instant smile, he buries his face between her legs again and feels her pressing down on him from above, holding him in place with both hands, rocking her hips forward hard against his tongue. She has a difficult time murmuring the word, "Green," and he has a harder time leaving that warmth, the delicious feast, and sitting upright again. But he does.

The tables are turned again. Molly is now the winner. He can tell from her smirk that she's got a few things planned once they stop. That is, if they miss the last light. It turns yellow as he cruises through, and he doesn't bother to meet her gaze.

They both know what yellow means....

They turn at a stop sign and park beneath a pepper tree, and Jason motions for Molly to get out of the car. She smiles as she does, moving quickly. As he gets out of his side and walks around to her, she turns quickly, facing the car and offering him her ass—her beautiful, perfect, heart-shaped ass. Jason grabs her around the waist, not checking to see if she's wet enough. He can smell her scent from where he stands. He thrusts forward, entering her instantly, and they begin a new ride. Beat for beat, her hips swivel against his, and her breathing catches each time he pushes forward.

She tries to regain her balance by leaning against the car, but he lifts her off her feet and pulls her back down on him, impaling her on his cock. How she sighs when she feels him inside, how she moans when he finds that perfect spot within the tight walls of her pussy, the pleasure spot that takes her to a higher level.

As the ride escalates, she calls out his name, bucking against him wildly. She fucks like that only when she is really turned on: aggressively, dominantly, even with him behind her. It makes his cock grow harder to feel her pulling at him, squeezing with the powerful muscles of her pussy.

Before he knows what is going on, she pulls off him and turns, face-to-face, motioning with a flick of her coal black hair for him to switch places. He does, without speaking, and she comes into his arms and then nearly climbs his body, straddling his rock-hard cock, wrapping her legs around his waist.

"Now," she says, moving him against the car, pounding into him, the blush of her cheeks caused by lust, not embarrassment; the glow in her eyes pure and simple, golden in the fading light, violet with the heat of it all.

"Yes," he says, more of a sigh, a whisper, than a spoken word. "Oh, yes, Molly, yes."

They come together, holding each other, moving back and forth with the rhythmic pounding of their climaxes. There is a sweet, soft breeze that picks up around them, stirring leaves and fallen flower petals in a gently fragrant whirlwind. They can smell the ocean. They can smell the heat of their bodies and the silver scent of their sex, mingling. Jason's arms are tight around her body, and for a frozen moment it seems as if he'll never let her go.

But then a car pulls down the street, and they hurry to get into the VW, to hide themselves in the flurry of dressing. As Molly pulls her dress over her head, she smiles at him. "I like that best," she says, crashed out beside him, reaching for his hand.

"What?"

"I like it when the game works out like that."

He grins at her and strokes a wispy curl away from her glistening cheek. And together they say, "A tie."

15 | NAUGHTY KNICKERS AND CLEVER COSTUMES

Dress Your Inner Slut

Brevity is the soul of lingerie.
—Dorothy Parker

Whether your favorite undergarments are frilly ruffled panties or silk boxers, what goes on beneath your clothes can be just as important as what you put on top. Or maybe even more so.

In "Fancy Pants" by Barbara Pizio, the narrator waxes poetic about his girlfriend's panties:

Fiona's dresser drawers are overflowing with sexy undergarments: lacy little thongs, silk string bikinis and soft cotton panties. I love how smooth and shapely her ass looks in tight pants when she's wearing a thong. And she's always adorable lounging about on Sunday morning in her floral-print cotton panties. *But I must confess that my personal favorite is a pair of black mesh boy-cut briefs with three horizontal lines of tiny pink ruffles that adorn her best feature—her ass.*

Fiona's lush cheeks peek out of the bottom of those short-shorts in the sexiest way. They're a fleshy tease just waiting to be slapped. I could spank her for hours, content to watch her soft flesh jiggle and jump each time my hand connects with her bottom.

The corset described in Donna George Storey's "Fezziwig's Balls" completely transforms the main character:

With a nervous smile, she lowered her arms. Madame wrapped the corset around Claire's torso and quickly fastened the clasps in front. Then she circled behind to tighten the laces. With each tug, Claire felt her chest move forward and up in response. The corset seemed to embrace her, meld itself to her skin, squeezing her breath and her flesh vertically so that she felt inches taller.

She also felt an undeniable twinge of pleasure between her legs.

"It's not too tight, is it?" Madame asked, her voice almost a whisper.

"No, it's fine," Claire responded, her own voice faint and breathless.

A full vixen outfit gives the girl power in Saskia Walker's "Skin on Skin":

A cutoff latex top, sleeveless and skintight, left her midriff bare. A leather miniskirt was cinched around her hips, zippered from waist to hem at front and back. Shiny soft plastic boots clung to her legs, like skins on her skin. The decadent outfit gave her cover; it also gave her nerve.

High-heeled boots do the trick in Shanna Germain's "Puss-in-Boots":

In the end, I chose the black wraparound dress, nothing under it but me. I slid it on before he got home, tied it loosely around my waist. Then I pulled the boots up over my ankles and calves. The leather curved perfectly around my calves and stopped just below the knee. I could barely walk in the heels, but I figured it didn't matter: If I could just knock his eyes out when he walked in the door, I'd be okay.

While stockings hold all the power in Rachel Kramer Bussel's "Fishnet Queen":

Her legs are long, and in her miniskirt, which rides up her thigh, I can see her pale skin augmented by the tightly woven black pattern that seems made just for her. She doesn't just wear the fishnets, she owns them.

But if clothes make the man, then costumes make the couple—in bed and out. Minor additions can add up to erotic explosions if you practice a little creativity. You don't need to break your bank to bolster your libido. You only need a swift imagination. My simple rule is this: if you are playing out a fantasy, ask yourself, *What would I do to make this scene come to life?*

In "Knuckling Under," for example, Shanna Germain wrote about hot sex with a bike mechanic:

My orgasm was as fast and hard as his fingers, rushing through me and then gone. He kept his fingers in, let me spasm around him until my body was still.

When he removed his fingers I felt empty, split open. I took my legs off his shoulders, surprised at how heavy they felt, how tired I was. The whole room smelled like grease and salt. I realized he was still dressed, that I'd hardly touched him. That he hadn't come.

I reached for his zipper, but he stopped my hands. His fingers were still wet from me.

"It's okay," he said. He put one finger on my ripped stocking

and ran it down to my calf. It left a glistening trail on the black. "I got just what I wanted. Plus, I have to go back and finish your bike."

To recreate the scene from Shanna Germain's story, you don't need grease or a wrench. You don't even need a bike. But in this case, I'd definitely fuck in front of a mirror, and preferably on the edge of the sink. To really get in the mood, though, I might go for the costume: nylons that I don't mind being ripped.

I wrote about a couple caught in a role-playing game in "The Super":

His wife-beater T-shirt caught my eye first. The tight-ribbed cotton showed off his muscular arms and broad chest. I turned slightly to look at him, my hand on the small copper mailbox key, my whole body still like a deer considering the chances of crossing the street safely. If he noticed me, would that be a good thing or a bad thing? The connection happened suddenly. His eyes made forceful contact with my legs, and I felt each moment as he took his time appraising my outfit: slim short skirt in classic Burberry "Nova" plaid, opaque black stockings, shiny patent leather penny loafers, and lace shirt with a Johnny collar that was probably a bit too sheer for work, but I paired it with a skimpy peach-colored camisole and nobody said anything. Maybe somebody should have.

He did.

"Wore that to work today, did you?"

I blushed, instantly, automatically, and pretended there was dire importance in the action of checking my mail. My fingers felt slippery on the multitude of magazines and catalogs stuffed inside the tiny box, and I hoped I wouldn't drop the whole handful of mail. I could feel him moving closer, and now I could smell him, as well. Some masculine scent, mentholated shaving cream, or aftershave. Not cologne. That wouldn't be his style.

His hands were on me now, thick fingers smoothing the collar of the shirt, then caressing the nape of my neck, his thumb running up and down until I leaned my head back against his large hand. Crazy, right? In the lobby of the apartment building, letting this man touch me. But I couldn't help myself.

"A little slutty," he said, "don't you think?"

What would a story like this require? A white T-shirt. A too-sexy-for-work outfit. A leather belt.

That's all I needed in order for Sam to pounce and rip my...I mean, that's all *you'd* need to change a fantasy to reality.

EROTIC FICTION

THE DEATH OF THE MARABOU SLIPPERS

Molly Laster

F eathers. Pink-tipped white feathers.

The feathers transformed the shoes from any other innocent pair of bedroom slippers into true decadence. But maybe they weren't quite so innocent to start with. Maybe they knew what they were doing all along. You've seen the type—smug in their open-toedness. Willful in their daring high-heeled glory. Deliciously trimmed with a bit of tender white-pink marabou fluff on the front, just to get your attention.

I'd never owned shoes like these before. Sure, I'd seen versions of them in the Frederick's of Hollywood catalog, insolently positioned with toe toward the camera, daring the casual pursuer to purchase them. And I'd even drooled over such fantasy footwear when worn by my favorite forties screen stars: Myrna Loy, Claudette Colbert, Garbo. But those women had the clothes to go with the shoes—angel-sleeved nightgowns with three-foot trains, tight satin slips with plunging necklines. Such sexy slippers weren't meant for someone like me—a girl who owns plain white bra-and-panty sets, who wears Gap sweats to bed, whose one experience with a pair of black fishnets was a comedic disaster.

What purpose could a pair of wayward shoes like these possibly have?

Still, when I caught sight of the immoral mules at a panty sale in San Francisco, I bought them. Even though they were a size eight and I'm a size six. Even though I found the very sight of them fairly wicked. Even though my own bedroom slippers at home were made of plaid flannel and had been chewed on repeatedly by my golden retriever puppy.

I simply thought Lucas would like them.

He did.

"I'm gonna fuck those shoes," he said when I pulled them from the silver bag. "Sweetheart, those shoes are history."

I'd never seen him react like that to anything. My tall, handsome, green-eyed husband has a healthy libido. I definitely get my share of bedroom romping time. But as far as kinkiness goes, he has always appeared positively fetish free. No requests for handcuffs. No need for teddies or "special" outfits to get him in the mood. No urgent trips to Safeway at midnight for whipped cream, chocolate sauce, and maraschino cherries.

"Put them on," Lucas hissed. "Now."

I kicked off my patent leather penny loafers, pulled off my black stockings, and slid into the marabou mules. The white bit of fluff on the toes made the shoes look like some sort of pastry, a fantasy confection created just for feet. My red toenails peeked through the opening.

Dirty, I thought. *Indecent.*

Lucas got on the floor and kissed my exposed toes, stroked the soft feathery tips of the shoes, then stood and quickly shed his outfit.

"They're bad," he said excitedly, positioning himself over my feet as if preparing to do push-ups. He's ex-military and has excellent formation for this activity—his body becomes stiff and boardlike. The sleek muscles in his back shift becomingly under his tan skin. In this position, his straining cock went directly between the two mules.

"Oh, man," he whispered. "So bad they're good."

He went up and down over my shoes, digging his cock between them, dragging it over the marabou trim, sighing with delight when the feathers got between his legs. I could only imagine how those pale white feathers tickled his most sensitive organ.

"They're so soft," he murmured.

I'd been staring down at him, at his fine ass—clenching with each depraved push-up—at his strong back, the muscles rippling. Now, I looked straight ahead, into the full-length mirror across the room, taking in the total effect of our afternoon of debauchery.

I was fully dressed: long black skirt, black mock turtleneck, my dark hair in a refined ponytail, small spectacles in place. If you ended the reflection at my shins, you might have placed me for exactly what I am, an editor at an educational publishing company. Below my shins, however, was Lucas, doing ungodly push-ups over my brand-new shoes. My slim ankles were bare, feet sliding slightly in the too-big marabou-trimmed mules. If you disregarded the shoes, and imagined Lucas moving in stop-frame animation, he might have been culled from a series of Eadweard Muybridge pictures. But with the shoes in place, and with Lucas's body moving rigidly up and down, this picture looked more like something from a fantastic pornographic movie.

I stared at our images and felt myself growing more and more aroused. My plain white panties were suddenly too containing. My skirt and sweater needed to come off. Arousal rushed through me in a shuddering wave. But I kept my peace—this wasn't my fantasy, wasn't my moment. It was Lucas's. All his.

He began speaking louder, first lauding the shoes, "Sweet, so sweet." Then criticizing the slippers as he slammed between them, "Oh, you're bad...bad."

I stayed as still as possible, watching in awe as Lucas, approaching his limit, arched up and sat back on his heels, his hand working his cock in double-time. Small bits of pure white feathers were stuck to the sticky tip of his swollen penis. More feather fluffs floated in the air around us.

"Give me one of the shoes," he demanded, and I kicked off the right slipper. One hand still wrapped around his cock, he used the other to lift the discarded shoe and began rubbing the tip of it between his legs, moaning and sighing, his words no longer intelligible, no longer necessary. Then, suddenly, as if inspiration had hit him, he reached behind his body with the shoe, poking the heel of it between the cheeks of his ass, impaling himself with the slipper while he dragged the tip of his cock against the shoe I still wore.

I watched closely as his breathing caught, as he leaned back farther still and then came, ejaculating on the slipper before him, coating those naughty feathers with semen, matting the feathers into a sticky mess. Showing them once and for all who was boss.

When he had relaxed enough to speak, he looked up at me, a sheepish expression on his face. "Told you those shoes were history," he said, red-cheeked. Embarrassed. "Told you, baby, didn't I?"

I just nodded, thinking: The death of an innocent pair of marabou slippers. What'd the shoes ever do to Lucas? Nothing but exist.

PRETTY AS A PICTURE | 16

Smile for the Camera

Anything that excites me for any reason, I will photograph; not searching for unusual subject matter, but making the commonplace unusual.
—Edward Weston

Are you ready for your close-up? Of course you are! Lovers sometimes forget exactly how powerful playing with a camera can be. What can you do aside from emulating the style of those 1950s-style Vargas pinups? So many things that you won't believe it once you start. Polaroids—if you can find the film. Digital. Video. Once you begin, you might not be able to stop. At least, that's how it is for me and Sam. The first time was for work. He took pictures of me for a poster for one of his plays—arranged me just so. I was wet before he started, just from the arranging.

"Take pictures of me," I begged after. "Forget the props."

He took Polaroids, the poses getting more dangerous with each shot. He spread them over me while we fucked.

The video camera came next. First we just fucked for the camera. Then we moved on to watching the video of ourselves while we screwed. I can hardly describe the sensation I felt, being part of that kinky loop—unending, unrelenting.

As our relationship's grown, so has the age of digital toys. Sam can take pictures of me with his phone now; make movies on the computer and upload the movies to…well, no. Not yet. Not really. Not us. But you can see where this is going, right? If you're interested in having a peek at what other people do with a camera, check out all of the amateur porn on YouPorn.com. Every day, there are brand-new videos of people just like you making their own X-rated movies.

Teresa Lamai's "Small Windows" further explains the power of being videoed:

Fuck. I don't know when he turned the recorder on. He's left the monitor turned toward me. The last rays of sunset, pale apricot and scarlet, fall in stripes over the rumpled bed. My naked body is overexposed, gleaming sickly white in the blue-tinted screen. I don't recognize myself; my breasts are rounds of delicate mushroom flesh; my cunt a glistening, dark-furred maw. The screen is like an opening into a smaller, more vivid world, thick with black-green air, where an unfamiliar woman has let herself be drawn into view. He knew I'd be helpless to look away.

In "The Secret to a Happy Marriage" by Rachel Kramer Bussel, a couple at a sex party uses a video camera to give a little thrill to an already fairly thrilling situation:

One time they set up a little corner "booth," where they took turns bending over for anyone who chose to spank them with their choice of implements. They bring a huge toy bag that sometimes has a video camera, and they've been known to get someone to tape them fucking, then gift the cameraman or woman with the tape, like a naughty goodie bag prize.

And in Mike Kimera's "Have a Nice Day," when she least expects it, the main character is shown a video of herself being fucked:

As you scramble for balance you hear the sound of yourself coming. The video in the limo shows you being fucked by me and coming hard.

"Don't just lie there, Jenny, take a seat and watch the show— I've seen it twice. By the way, my name's Lily." You look up and then past her and finally you see me sitting in the center of a bench seat. I look at you but say nothing.

Of course, if you're not ready to make your own movies yet, you can always get off watching those made by the experts, or watching your lover watch the movies, as in Heidi Champa's "Lights Out":

You reach for the remote to turn off the video, but I interrupt you.

"Leave it on. Don't let me stop you."

I flick off the lights, and settle into the armchair opposite the couch. I can't see the television, but I can see you. You look from me to the screen and back. Unsure, you start moving your hand down your cock, slowly. The blue glow shows me your eyes, looking at me, seeing me stare. I've never watched you before. I like it.

Back and forth your eyes jump between me and the screen. Soon, your eyes close, just for a minute. I hear a little grunt come out of your mouth, and your tongue darts across your bottom lip. I settle my hand into my panties, feeling wet from seeing you this way.

Or, if all of this is a bit out of your league or comfort range, why not simply have good old-fashioned sex at a movie theater, as occurs in my story "Ancient History":

I don't know how you and I made the connection in the dark balcony of that dilapidated theater—but we did. I knew you'd seen me, because you kept turning around to check me out. I learned the look of your face in that odd blue glow of the flickering celluloid. At the first intermission, you asked my name. At the second, you held my hand for a moment, squeezing my fingertips as you got me to tell you about myself. After the final movie, when it was too late to call it late anymore, and too early to call it dawn, we went out behind the theater to the overly graffiti-adorned alley, and you pressed me up against the wall and kissed me.

You can devote entire scenarios to being photographed or taking pictures—or let the cameras or videos become simply sex toys, part of a scene without dominating the show. Whatever you decide, your evening is sure to be rated XXX.

PICTURE PERFECT

Donna George Storey

I didn't mean to shave it all off. At first I was trying for a whimsical heart shape, but I couldn't seem to get the curves even. Then I sculpted a fur patch like those models in men's magazines, but it looked too much like Hitler's mustache. In the end I went all the way—the Greek statue look. It's harder than you think to get yourself all smooth down there. I stood with one leg propped up on the side of the tub, studying my cunt like exam notes. I'd never looked at myself so carefully down there before. What surprised me was the color—the deep, almost shocking pink of the inner lips. The skin looked so sensitive and dewy, I was scared to get close with that nasty razor, so I left a little fringe. There was no room for mistakes.

I called Brian at work to tell him about my art project.

"Hey, Kira." I knew someone was in his office by his offhand tone, but I went ahead and told him anyway.

"I just shaved my pussy."

There was a pause.

"Oh, is that so? Listen, honey, I'm in the middle of a meeting right now. I'll call you back when I can. Okay?" Only a wife would have picked up the faint tremor in his voice.

Unfortunately, Brian was a model employee—not the type who would stand up in front of the boss and announce, "Sorry, I have to go. My wife just shaved her pussy." It would probably be hours before he could get home. That left a whole afternoon alone, just me and my bald snatch.

I went over to the full-length mirror. My heart was pounding. I hadn't felt this naughty since I was a teenager doing "homework" up in my bedroom with my panties around one ankle and a pillow pushed between my legs, ear cocked for the sound of my mother's footsteps in the hall. Which was silly because I was alone in my own house and all I was doing was looking at myself, my new self: the white triangle of smooth skin, the fold of tender pink flesh now visible between the lips. There was an indentation at the top of the slit, as if someone had pressed a finger into it. I had an overwhelming urge to play with myself. Just an appetizer before I jumped Brian's bones tonight. I touched a tentative finger to my clit. I was already wet.

The phone rang.

"I'm taking the afternoon off," Brian told me. His voice was husky. "I'll be home in twenty minutes. Don't you dare touch that shaved pussy of yours until I get there."

When I hung up, I had to smile. My husband knew me well. Very well.

There were no hi-honey kisses or how-was-your-day's; the moment Brian got through the door, he pushed me back on the sofa and yanked open my robe. He made a little sound in his throat, half gasp, half moan.

"Wow, you really did a job on it."

I smiled. "Didn't you believe me?"

He gaped, eyes glowing. *Pussy power*—suddenly the words took on fresh meaning. Gently he nudged my thighs apart. I shivered. He bent down. I thought—and hoped—he was going to kiss me there.

"You didn't get all the hair off."

"Hey, it's a tricky job."

He frowned. "Don't move."

He left me lying on the sofa with my legs spread like a virgin sacrifice. My pussy was getting chilly, but my breath was coming fast and I had that naughty teenage feeling again, arousal so sharp it was almost pain.

Brian returned with a towel, a canister of shaving cream and a razor. He'd changed into his bathrobe, which did nothing to hide his bobbing erection. He came back again with a basin of water, which he set carefully on the coffee table. The last trip brought the video camera and tripod.

I felt a contraction low in my belly.

"Spread your legs wider."

I caught my breath, but obeyed.

He patted a dab of shaving cream between my legs. The coolness made me squirm.

"Lie still."

He was acting awfully bossy, but I didn't want any slipups. I held my thighs to keep them from shaking.

"Relax, Kira," Brian said, more kindly. Guys are always saying that when they're about to mess around with your private parts. Still Brian did have plenty of experience with shaving, so I closed my eyes and took a deep breath. The room was quiet, except for scraping sound of razor and the occasional swish of water. At last he rinsed me with a washcloth, smiling as I wriggled under his vigorous assault.

He leaned close to examine his work.

"Picture perfect," he declared.

Five minutes later, I was sitting naked in our armchair, watching my own twat, larger than life on our new plasma TV screen. My legs were modestly pressed together, but Brian had me lounge back so you could see the slit, shorn of its covering. He knelt, pointing the camera straight at me.

"Did you get turned on when you were shaving?" His tone was soothing now, like a friendly interviewer on a weekly news magazine.

"Yes," I admitted in a small voice.

"Did you masturbate?"

"No." A few flicks didn't count, right?

"You wanted to, though."

I swallowed.

Brian clicked his tongue. "Why don't you do it now? Don't you want to know if it feels different when it's shaved?"

My face burned, but I ignored the question and turned to the screen. "It sure looks different."

"Yeah. It really does look like lips. The skin gets pinker here and pouts." He reached over and pinched the edges.

I bit back a moan.

"We could put lipstick on it. Deep red like a forties movie star."

"No, that's too weird," I said and immediately regretted it. Why was I being such a prude? After all, I'd started this with my little experiment in the tub. Suddenly bold, I glided my middle finger up and down along the groove. "This is an easier way to make it redder."

Brian grinned. "Yes, indeed. Let's get the full view." The camera zoomed in expectantly.

I hesitated. I'd played with myself in front of Brian before, but now a stranger was in the room with us, a stranger with a round, staring eye.

"Go ahead, honey. I know you're turned on. Your chest is all flushed."

I inched my thighs open, glancing at the TV. To my embarrassment I was already quite ruddy down there and shiny-slick with pussy juice. The fleshy folds and hole filled up the screen. My finger, laboring at my clit, looked strangely small.

"Does it feel different?" Brian was back to being the cordial journalist.

"A little."

"Tell me."

"The mound is really smooth, like satin."

"Is it more sensitive?"

"Yes, I think so. The outer lips are tingling. Or maybe I'm just noticing it more." I looked up at him. "What's with all the questions? You sound like you're interviewing my pussy for a dirty documentary."

Brian laughed. "What if I was?"

"Now wait a minute." I sat up and snapped my legs together.

He turned the camera to my face. A frowning twin gazed back at me from the TV.

Brian, on the other hand, was still smiling. "What if there was a guy in the city, a dot-com billionaire, who collects videos of married ladies pleasuring themselves?"

My pulse jumped. "You're joking right?"

"For his eyes only, discretion guaranteed. He pays well for it."

"Oh, yeah? How much?"

"Three grand for a genuine orgasm. That won't be a problem for you. We might get even more because you're all shaved down there. Just think, Kira, we could go on a nice vacation for a few very pleasant minutes of work."

I moaned and covered my face with my hands.

"Don't worry. I'll edit this part out. He specifically requested no faces. Just sweet pussy."

Would my own husband really sell some rich voyeur a movie of me masturbating? I never thought he had it in him. And I never thought I'd find the idea so fiercely arousing. Funny all the things you discover when you shave your pussy.

Brian put the camera on stand-by. His eyes twinkled. "Jake and Ashley did it."

"No way."

"Lie back. I'll tell you about it."

There was my pussy on the screen again; there I was, a sprawled-legged Aphrodite, her naughty parts tinted dark rose.

"Ashley let Jake talk her into this?"

"Better than that. She went with him to drop it off. The guy tacks on a bonus if the lady and her husband join him for a drink."

I pictured Brian's best friend's wife, with her spiky blonde hair and lip ring, swishing up the stairs of a mansion in a black party dress and heels. That wasn't so hard to believe. "What was the rich guy like? I bet he was a creep."

"Jake said he was the perfect gentleman. Fortyish. Friendly. He served them a glass of champagne and hors d'oeuvres made by his personal chef. They chatted a bit, then left with an envelope of cash. Easiest money they ever made."

"I don't think I could meet him." So why did I see myself walking up those same mansion steps, Brian at my side, video in hand? I wasn't as wild as Ashley. I'd have on something prim: a lace blouse, a velvet choker with a cameo, a long skirt. I'd wear my hair up and keep my eyes down, blushing under his billion-dollar gaze. The perfect lady. That rich guy would get a boner the size of Florida just looking at me.

"Jake said the guy only did one thing that crossed the line. When they were leaving he took Ashley's right hand and kissed it like he was a baron or something."

"What's wrong with kissing her hand?" I had a weakness for old-fashioned manners.

"Well, it's the hand she uses to masturbate, of course. Like you're doing right now."

Without my realizing it, my hand had wandered back down between my legs. I jerked it away.

Brian laughed. Holding the camera steady, he reached up and guided my fingers back to my pussy. "Don't be bashful, honey. He wants to watch you do it. So do I."

And the truth was, I wanted them to see, the two pairs of eyes floating before me: Brian's the greenish gray of a northern sea, the rich guy's golden and glittering.

"Where does he watch it? In his home theater?" Under the veil of my lashes I studied the screen. My labia jiggled lewdly as my finger strummed on. That's what the rich guy would see as he sat on his leather couch in his silk dressing gown. A wine-colored gown, the same color as his swollen dick. He'd pull it out and stroke it as he watched.

"A home theater, yes," Brian said softly. "State of the art."

"Why are you doing this? Don't you care if your wife shows her cunt to some horny billionaire?" The words came in gasps.

"The joke's on him. We'll take his money and get a suite in the fanciest hotel in town and fuck all night." Brian sounded winded, too, as if he'd just finished a run. Then I realized he was jerking off.

"I'm not a whore." I was half-sobbing, from shame and pleasure.

"Of course you're not, honey. You're a nice, pretty married lady. That's what he wants. Someone he'd glimpse at the gourmet grocery store or the espresso bar, buying a nonfat decaf cappuccino. I see guys staring at you. If only they knew the truth about my sweet-faced angel. If only they knew you want it so bad you shave your pussy and let men take pictures of it."

Sounds were coming out of my throat, sounds I'd never made before, high-pitched whines and animal moans.

"You're the hottest thing he's ever seen, but no matter how much he pays he can never have the real you."

"Oh, god, I'm gonna come," I whimpered.

A hand closed around my wrist and wrenched it away.

"He'll pay an extra thousand if you come while we fuck."

"Did Ashley do it?" I panted. I knew what the answer would be.

"Jake said she had the best orgasm of her life."

Brian hurriedly fixed the camera to the tripod, adjusted the height, then lifted me to my feet and took my place on the chair.

"Face the camera," he said.

My knees were as soft as melted caramel, but by gripping the arms of the chair I managed to position myself properly. On the screen Brian's penis reared up, my smooth snatch hovering above.

"Sit on it."

I lowered myself onto him with a sigh. Then I was up again, a woman who couldn't make up her mind. Up or down? It was there in full color: Brian's rod plunging in and out, his balls dangling beneath like a small pink pillow.

"Now turn around and ride me."

In a daze I straddled him, my knees digging into the cushion. Just last week, we'd done it this way on the sofa. We pretended it was prom night and we were sneaking a midnight quickie while my parents snored in the bedroom upstairs.

"Do you like to fuck with a shaved twat?"

"Yes," I confessed. "I like to rub my bare lips on you." Which was exactly what I was doing, lingering on the downstroke to grind my exposed clit against the rough hairs at the base of his cock.

"You're so wet. That rich guy can hear it. Your hungry wet lips gobbling up my cock."

Brian began to twist my nipples between his fingers.

"It's an extra five hundred if you show him your asshole."

I grunted assent and bucked harder. In that position, the rich guy could see it anyway. Then he whispered in my ear, "And another five hundred if you let me touch it."

I froze midthrust. "Please, Brian, don't," I whispered back. I didn't want the rich guy to hear. We'd recently discovered that when Brian diddles my butt crack when we fuck, it feels like a second clit. I loved it, but I wanted my little perversion to be our secret. Brian knew he could make me blush just talking about it.

"Why not, baby? Because he'll know you're a bad girl who comes when I play with your pretty ass?"

"Please," I begged. My asshole, however, seemed to have other ideas, the brazen little show-off, pushing itself out, all plumped and ticklish.

"Please what, Kira? I know you want it, but I won't touch it until you say yes."

"Please," I gasped. "Yes."

"That's a good girl. Nice and polite."

Good girl, bad girl, I wasn't sure what I was, but it didn't matter. My torso rippled like a column of heat between his hands, one tweaking my nipple, the other going to town on my quivering bottom. Our bodies made rude noises, swampy, squishy sounds—or was it the rich guy whacking off? He probably used a special custom-made lotion to make his dick all slippery. He'd be close to the end now, pumping his fist faster and faster, his single nether eye weeping a tear of delight. He'd gotten everything he wanted. The cool lady in the gourmet grocery store was unzipped and undone, a bitch in heat, writhing shamelessly on her husband's cock for his viewing pleasure.

But I had one little surprise left for him.

"What if you spank it? Is that another thousand?"

"Two thousand." I could tell Brian was close, too.

"I want him to see it. Spank my naughty asshole," I yelled, so the rich guy could hear.

The first slap sent a jolt straight through me that quickly dissolved into pleasure, foamy fingers of a wave creeping into the hollows of my body.

"Again."

Smack.

Each blow hammered me deeper onto Brian's cock. I pushed my ass out to take the next one, to show that rich guy I could do it. He was so turned on, I could feel his eyes burning into my back through the screen. But it wasn't just him. There were others watching—my parents, my high school science teacher, the postal clerk who sneaks glances at my tits, a Supreme Court justice or two—dozens of them, their faces twisted into masks of shock and fascination. And beneath, in the shadows, hands were stroking hard-ons or shoved into panties that were damp and fragrant with arousal. They liked it, all of them, and I was watching them as they watched me in an endless circle of revelation and desire.

"I'm...gonna...come."

"Come for him. Now!" Brian bellowed. The last slaps fell like firecrackers snapping, and I jerked my hips to their rhythm as my climax tore through my belly. With the chair springs squeaking like crazy and Brian grunting, "Fuck your shaved pussy, fuck it," that rich guy got himself quite a show.

I'd say it was worth every penny.

Afterward, I pulled Brian down to the carpet with me. Our profiles filled the screen. He'd seen me and I'd seen him and we fit so well together and I loved him more than anything. I told him that. Or maybe I just kissed him, a deep soul kiss that lasted a long, long time.

The rich guy got that part for free.

17 | CUE THE QUICKIE

We're Going to Be Late!

Smile at each other, make time for each other.
—**Mother Teresa**

Don't Have Time for Sex" may truly be my favorite *type* of sex. When I'm all dolled up and on my way out the door, and Sam says, "Hey, where are *you* going?" I instantly get wet. Or when the company is about to arrive, the water is about to boil, the conference call is about to begin, *that's* when our lust flames brightest.

Don't believe me? Here's what happened the other night:

"We're going to be late," I told him as I stepped into the kitchen.

"Who said you could look like that?"

That was his response. Not "Let's go." Not "Here's your

coat, honey." But: "Who said you could look like that?"

I glanced down: black Blondie T-shirt—Debbie Harry's image on the front, *One Way or Another* on the back—sheer black cardigan. Triple-strand necklace of faux pearls and shiny obsidian beads. Favorite skirt, a cascade of black and white with ruffles. Black kick-ass boots with chrome hardware. He hadn't seen the stockings yet. Or the panties.

"Who said?" he asked one more time, voice low.

I didn't know how to answer that. Well, I did, I guess. I mean, I *thought* I did.

"Lift your skirt."

I lifted my skirt.

"Oh, baby," he whispered. "Who said you could wear fish-nets?"

My cheeks were flushed. We were late already, supposed to be at a dinner party, an anniversary party for longtime friends. If he did what I thought he was going to do, started what I guessed he was going to start, we were going to be even later.

"Higher."

I lifted my skirt higher.

"Who said you could wear those panties?"

I was wearing red lace boy shorts, beautiful panties I wear only on special occasions. He stepped closer to me, put one hand on the front of the knickers and whispered, "Who said you could be wet like that?"

I sucked in my breath, looked at him, remembered all of the effort I had put into getting dressed, considered what I was going to look like by the time we were through—cheeks flushed fuchsia, stockings ripped, red Russet Moon lipstick smeared. Only seconds had passed, but I felt as if not my whole life, but our whole evening, had run through my head. The conversations we would have at the dinner party, me with my panties either drenched or gone, my heart still racing from the thrill of our five-minute fuck.

Because this *is* his favorite time to play, as well. When there *is* no time.

Was it kismet that I was working on the final chapter for this book when this encounter took place? Had he peered over my shoulder to sneak a peak at my table of contents? Or was he in my head when I got dressed, knowing that if he caught a glimpse of the fishnets, a sliver of the red lace panties, there would be no way we'd be able to arrive at the party before the main course. And perhaps not before dessert.

"Who said you could make me this hard?" he asked, and I grinned and stepped out of my panties, sure that we'd come up with excuses along the way.

DINNER'S READY

Alison Tyler

So he's fucking me in the kitchen and calling me Julia. And the fire alarm goes off as he starts spanking my ass. Wisps of smoke swirl around us and the light flashes on and off. My jeans and panties pool round my ankles. My long silver-streaked hair falls loose past my shoulders. I've got on an old blue hoodie over a favorite well-worn scarlet tee.

"Oh, Julia."

He's spanking my ass with something hard and whippy, plastic—but what?

"Fucking hell."

The alarm right above us keeps flashing and screaming.

"You feel so good."

I look down to see pink panties with little flowers, and I'm not wearing a bra under the shirt.

"Sweet Julia"

I smell the sweet sizzling smell of something burning.

"Jesus fucking Christ."

Now, I'm getting closer, and the smoke's getting thicker.

"That's such a slick sweet pussy."

He drops the dustpan—dustpan!—a laugh rises up in my throat.

"You get so wet for me."

Then slam-bam-wham, and we're done.

ABOUT THE CONTRIBUTORS

For more about the authors featured in this book, please visit their blogs or websites:

H. L. Berry: http://www.myspace.com/hlberry
Cheyenne Blue: http://cheyenneblue.com/
Rachel Kramer Bussel: http://rachelkramerbussel.com/
Heidi Champa: http://heidichampa.blogspot.com/
Erica DeQuaya: http://www.myspace.com/ericadequaya.
Dayle A. Dermatis: http://www.cyvarwydd.blogspot.com/
Bonnie Dee: http://bonniedee.com
Jeremy Edwards: http://jerotic.blogspot.com/
Emerald: http://www.myspace.com/emerald150
Ann Rosenquist Fee: http://www.annrosenquistfee.com/
Shanna Germain: http://yearofthebooks.wordpress.com/
P. S. Haven: http://www.myspace.com/pshaven
Michael Hemmingson: http://avantpop.livejournal.com/
Jolene Hui: http://jolenehui.blogspot.com/

Isabel Kerr: http://isabelkerr.blogspot.com/
Mike Kimera: http://mikekimera.blogspot.com/
D. L. King: http://www.dlkingerotica.com
Kis Lee: http://www.kislee.net/
Marilyn Jaye Lewis: http://marilynjayelewis.com/
Fiona Locke: http://fionalocke.net/
Kristina Lloyd: http://kristinalloyd.wordpress.com/
Mathilde Madden: http://www.mathildemadden.co.uk/
Nikki Magennis: http://nikkimagennis.blogspot.com/
Sommer Marsden: http://smutgirl.blogspot.com
Gwen Masters: http://gwenmasters.com/
Aimee Nichols: http://www.intergalactic-hussy.net/
Elspeth Potter: http://www.victoriajanssen.com
Dakota Rebel: http://vampsmut.blogspot.com/
Thomas S. Roche: http://thomasroche.com/
Stephen D. Rogers: http://www.stephendrogers.com/
Craig J. Sorensen: http://just-craig.blogspot.com/
Donna George Storey: http://sexfoodandwriting.donnageorges-torey.com/
Saskia Walker: http://saskiawalker.co.uk/
Sharon Wachsler: http://www.sharonwachsler.com/
Rita Winchester: http://www.myspace.com/ritawinchester
Kristina Wright: http://www.kristinawright.com/

Note: Not all of the authors featured in this book have blogs or websites; information about their credits (and more about all of the writers in this book) will be posted on: http://neverhavethesamesextwice.blogspot.com/.

ABOUT
THE AUTHOR

Called a "trollop with a laptop" by *East Bay Express* and a "literary siren" by Good Vibrations, Alison Tyler has made being naughty her official trademark. Her sultry short stories have appeared in more than eighty anthologies including *Rubber Sex* (Cleis), *Dirty Girls* (Seal Press), and *Sex for America* (Harper Perennial). She is the author of more than twenty-five erotic novels, most recently *Melt with You* (Virgin), and the editor of more than forty-five explicit anthologies, including *J Is for Jealousy* (Cleis), *Naughty Fairy Tales from A to Z* (Plume), and *Naked Erotica* (Pretty Things Press).

Ms. Tyler is loyal to coffee (black), lipstick (red), and tequila (straight). She has tattoos, but no piercings; a wicked tongue, but a quick smile; and bittersweet memories, but no regrets. She believes it won't rain if she doesn't bring an umbrella, prefers hot and dry to cold and wet, and loves to spout her favorite motto: "You can sleep when you're dead." She chooses Led Zeppelin over the Beatles, the Cure over the Smiths, and the Stones over everyone—yet although she appreciates good rock, she has a pitiful weakness for '80s hair bands.

In all things important, she remains faithful to her partner of nearly fifteen years, but she still can't choose just one perfume. Find her on the web at www.alisontyler.com, or visit http://www. myspace.com/alisontyler if you want to be her friend.